ADOPT &

MICROSOFT TEAMS

A MANAGER'S GUIDE TO
COMMUNICATION, COLLABORATION, AND COORDINATION
WITH MICROSOFT TEAMS

Paul Woods, Helen Blunden, Benjamin Elias, & Darrell Webster

Foreword by
Karuana Gatimu, Microsoft Teams Engineering

Adopt & **Embrace**.

Published by Change Empire Books
https://www.changeempire.com

Printed on demand in Australia, United States and United Kingdom
Set in Palatino Linotype
Edited & designed by Change Empire Books

While the authors have made every effort to provide accurate internet addresses at the time of publication, neither the publisher nor the authors assume any responsibility for errors or for changes that occur after publication. Furthermore, the publisher does not have any control over and does not assume any responsibility for author or third-party websites or their content.

Adopt & Embrace Microsoft Teams is an independent publication and is neither affiliated with, nor authorised, sponsored, or approved by, Microsoft Corporation. All other trademarks are the property of their respective owners.

Paperback ISBN: 978-0-6487453-2-7
eBook ISBN: 978-0-6487453-0-3

To Kerrina, Gabby, and Maddy;

… to Andrew (you always told me to write a book, well, here it is);

… to Margaret, Noah, and Isabelle;

… to my dear wife Alicia and children, Ezekiel, Isaac, Eden, and Daniel. All my love and thanks for the years of support, inspiration, and understanding;

… and to the rest of the team at Adopt & Embrace
Nicole, Jenni, Jeff, John, and Maddy

Thank you for putting up with us as we brought this crazy idea to life

CONTENTS

FOREWORD

In Microsoft Teams Engineering, we have a simple goal—to make teamwork productive and enjoyable for all involved. The simplicity of this goal sometimes obscures its complexity. Achieving this—and the goal of empowering people and organisations around the world to achieve more of their own outcomes—drives us, both individually and as an organisation. We believe that you too want productive and enjoyable teamwork, and that may contribute to why you've picked up this text.

In my role running the Customer Advocacy Group, I have the privilege of meeting people from around the world, all of whom strive to use technology to accelerate the delivery of their objectives. They have many questions. What tools should I use? How do I manage Microsoft Teams? What about all our other technology? These are all valid questions, answers for which you can find in this book and in our core documentation at SuccessWithTeams.com. Yet, when I meet with these passionate, intelligent people, I encourage them to remember a key element of success: their employees. Teamwork, after all, is about *people*, not technology.

Microsoft Teams is nothing short of a transformative tool for productivity in your environment. We've been excited and humbled by the reactions of people from every type of organisation. Acting as a hub for teamwork, it brings together people, information, and powerful tools from within and outside of the Microsoft ecosystem. It strives to support your work in natural ways and to increase your enjoyment of your work along the way. But it is only as powerful as the people who use it. The success of any technology implementation rests in the hands of employees in all their variety. First-line information workers, executive and skilled alike, deserve a world-class employee experience on any device. Deciding to implement Microsoft Teams is a step towards delivering that experience, and the knowledge contained in this book can help you design it in a way that will inspire and delight.

As you go through this text and the innovative framework it contains, I'd encourage you to prioritise the needs of these employees in their differing forms. If you don't know their needs, conduct a simple survey or visit your virtual or real-world coffee room or watercooler and ask a few questions. In my experience as an Enterprise Service Adoption Specialist, I've come to understand that people will tell you what they need, if they are only asked. You may think certain features are of the utmost importance, only to determine that the needs of your team are more straightforward. In any scenario, Microsoft Teams, when paired with a mindful strategy, can improve collaboration, connection, and outcomes.

By its very nature, Microsoft Teams requires an iterative approach. The longer you use it, the more scenarios you'll be able to see that may be improved with its features. Integrating applications, creating tabs, communicating in channel conversations, and connecting Microsoft Teams to other line-of-business applications are additional capabilities that can pull together people and information in meaningful ways. The use of video in all your meetings, large and small, increases the quality of communication, which can lead to innovation and accelerated problem solving. Taking the given framework and applying it to your needs with an appropriate amount of flexibility will create the best experience. Keep suggested guardrails in place so that people across your organisation have an idea of how to collaborate in this new experience while recognising that their needs will change over time.

Utilising these capabilities together, centred around shared goals, can reduce context-switching across other experiences. This shared focus can aid in reducing change fatigue and the stressors too often encountered in the modern workplace. I believe that investing your time in what this book has to offer will speed you towards a streamlined experience that you and your employees deserve.

At Microsoft, we are here to help. Use this book and our online forums to gain knowledge, ask questions, and get inspiration from other travellers on this path. You can find me and many other members of our group on the Microsoft Technical Community in our Microsoft Teams forum (https://aka.ms/TeamsCommunity) and our site dedicated to driving adoption of all the services in Microsoft 365 (https://aka.ms/MicrosoftAdoption).

Reading this book is the beginning of a wonderful journey. Increasing collaboration and productivity is an evolution in human behaviour. When you prioritise the overall employee experience and the quality of your teamwork as a whole, we believe you will achieve your goals.

I want to take a moment to thank the authors—Paul, Helen, Benjamin, and Darrell—whose hard work has brought this text to life. Real-world guidance from talented people like these is essential for delivering on Microsoft's vision for the future of teamwork. Thank you for all you do for our community and its members!

Karuana Gatimu
Worldwide Office 365 Champion Program Lead
Principal Manager, Customer Advocacy Group
Microsoft Teams Engineering

PREFACE

It was the 14th of March, 2017, when things started to change. For most of the decade, organisations around the world had begun to embrace Microsoft's Office 365 to help their information or knowledge workers improve the way they work. Some organisations started by migrating their email to "the cloud," enabling their workforce to remove the shackles of a 200mb email inbox that had gotten in the way of doing things for years. Others started to shift away from their traditional S:\, T:\, or P:\ drive "network file shares" to an environment where more than one person could work on the same document at the same time. Simple changes when you write them on paper, but game-changing in the way it could influence how people and teams work together.

However, most organisations saw Office 365 as just a bundle of different tools. You would regularly hear trainers talk about "your toolkit," which contained different tools for different purposes. For example, you can use SharePoint for your team files, Skype for Business to communicate with your team using chat, audio, or video, or Planner to keep track of your tasks. This "toolkit" approach meant that your work was almost always spread across multiple silos in Office 365. As the complexity of your work increased, so did the cost of switching, or the mental gymnastics needed to keep up with where things were—or, dare I say it, "what tool to use when."

The day of March 14, 2017, changed all that. On the same day that the world's oldest golf club (Muirfield in Scotland) voted to admit women as members for the first time, and 52 sets of David Bowie stamps were launched into space, Microsoft Teams was unleashed on the world.

At *Adopt & Embrace*, we set Microsoft Teams up straight away and were blown away within minutes. As a distributed team, we rely heavily on video conferencing to keep us connected. When we saw the order of magnitude leap in the video experience compared to what we were used to with Skype for Business…we were hooked.

I was so excited, I took a photo and posted it to our company's Facebook and LinkedIn pages. You can see me gleefully taking a photo of our first Microsoft Teams experience on my Surface Pro (over Tim's shoulder) …

After about 30 minutes of playing with Microsoft Teams, we knew this could change the way that teams across the world could embrace technology to improve how they work every day. It took us a while to figure out exactly how, though. As a team, we continued to experiment and agreed on a simple approach that enabled us to better manage the way we collaborated and coordinated our customer work. The resulting improvement in the way we captured and shared knowledge and worked together to achieve better outcomes for our customers had a meaningful impact on our business.

It was at that time that our customers started to realise the potential positive impact on their businesses that could take place by rethinking business processes and work practices using Microsoft Teams. A true digital workspace where we can communicate about, collaborate on, and coordinate our work is now possible. A "single pane of glass" that allows us to better manage our workday is achievable, as is the ability to remove constraints of legacy IT infrastructure that stops us from being more mobile and closer to our customers. Chances are, if you're reading this book, that moment for you is today.

Why Did We Write This Book?

While we saw early versions of Microsoft Teams (under a non-disclosure agreement months before it was publicly released) and could see the potential of how, if used well, it could help transform how teams work together, it wasn't until we observed how our customers were taking their first steps—dipping their toes in the Microsoft Teams water—

that we noticed that more was necessary than just "Microsoft Teams training."

The early adopters jumped right in and started creating their own Teams. People defaulted to the familiar. "I work in the Marketing team; therefore, we need a 'Marketing Team'." "We are region X; therefore, we need a 'Region X Team'." The result was twofold—first, a somewhat messy list of Teams that loosely but didn't quite align to the organisational structure. Secondly, the realisation that nothing had changed, and almost all the Teams created simply duplicated the email distribution lists of the past. The problems with email overwhelm, or the challenges of poor work or organisational design were simply replicated in another system (with GIFs and emojis). There was no net gain in effectiveness or efficiency.

We knew that, without some guidance, what we sometimes call "bumper bowling"—guiderails that ensure you hit at least some (if not all) of the pins when you throw a bowling ball down a lane—would occur; most individuals, teams, and organisations looking to embrace new ways of working empowered by Microsoft Teams would likely not achieve the full outcome that they were seeking and would be unable to use Microsoft Teams to its full potential.

It is through iterative work with our customers over the past 18 months—helping them to navigate what seems like the age-old Microsoft Teams question: "How do I best set up my team?"—that we developed our *Adopt & Embrace* 10Ps of Microsoft Teams Design framework. It started out as just 3Ps—*Problem, Purpose,* and *People.* Those 3Ps could help anyone determine the right number of Teams to create for any organisational challenge they faced. We didn't want our customers trying to create one Team to solve every problem. We (together with our customers) saw the value in a more granular focus on the deliverable work. As we delved deeper into substantial use cases—like how best to structure a Team as a template for teaching and learning across an entire university; or how to structure a Team for more informal committee meetings; or how to connect first-line workers into their support offices—that we realised more nuance was required. The remaining seven Ps were slowly added to the framework. First it was *Priorities*, to help determine the right mix of channels to include. Then *Principles*, to help make sense of how we all agree to use the Team. *Plugins* came next, to guide how we add context and access to information or systems. This was followed by *Permissions*, to know who can do what and when, and *Performance*, so we know what success looks like. *Provisioning* came next, to determine the best way to get this collaboration and coordination space into the hands of the people who can generate value with it. And, finally, *Perishability*—what on earth do we do once we no longer need to use this Team?

We will be honest, *Perishability* started out as a bit of a joke (here is another random word that starts with P…because 10Ps sounds better than 9Ps); however, it has turned into one of the most important talking points we discuss with our customers—especially those who want to make sure they maximise the use and reuse of their intellectual property, those who want to ensure that their people are always learning, and IT departments who want to make sure that their Microsoft Teams environment does not suffer from unnecessary sprawl.

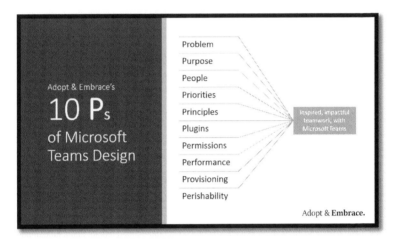

The reactions we saw from our customers when discussing the 10Ps framework were the inspiration to write this book. We could see that managers were struggling to make sense of how to best use Microsoft Teams to positively impact their people. They had a lot of questions but didn't have anywhere to start. IT Teams also couldn't neatly translate their understanding of how the product worked into something that made sense for their internal customers — HR, Marketing, Sales, Operations, Field Teams, Customer Service. Enter the 10Ps framework and this book.

At *Adopt & Embrace*, one of our core values is "always paying it forward." We couldn't just keep the 10Ps framework for the (relative) handful of customers we work with in Australia and New Zealand. We wanted this idea to spread across the world, which is why this book was born.

At *Adopt & Embrace*, as a Microsoft 2018 Global Partner of the Year, we recognise that, as a business, we should aspire to have a positive impact on a global scale. The best way to do that (ironically) is not through the latest and greatest technology like Microsoft Teams, but through one of the most ancient and most accessible technologies we have available: a book.

We hope that the ideas we develop in this book empower you to apply Microsoft Teams in new and innovative ways to help you better serve your customers; help you create a better employee experience; and, help you make a positive impact.

Paul Woods
Founder, Adopt & Embrace

INTRODUCTION

"Great…another collaboration tool. Don't we have sixteen other collaboration tools already? Email, desk phone, mobile phone, shared drives, the document spaces on our intranet, audio bridges, video conferencing, virtual meetings…even the water cooler in the kitchen. The list goes on! Why do we need a seventeenth?"

Good question. The short answer is no, you probably don't need a seventeenth collaboration tool.

The longer answer is that more technology tools will not improve the way your team works. Instead, *how* your team uses the tools at your fingertips to do their work is far more important.

The even longer answer is that if you have a tool at your fingertips that helps remove the barriers between all those different collaboration tools, work can be even better!

Chances are, if you've picked up this book, you have that tool at your fingertips: Microsoft Teams. Maybe your IT team has just "launched" Microsoft Teams to your team and the rest of your organisation. Maybe one of your new starters is "demanding" Microsoft Teams be set up because they used it at their previous employer. Maybe you overheard someone in the airline lounge or on the plane talking about how Microsoft Teams has helped them get their Outlook inbox under control and their team achieve more.

Whichever way Microsoft Teams landed in your work life, the fact that you are curious enough to open up this book means that you want to learn more, and, more importantly, figure out how you can use Microsoft Teams to make your (and your team's) life much easier. This can help you achieve your professional goals, like hitting your KPIs, and your personal goals, like getting your lunch break back and getting out of the office on time.

Right now, you likely have several questions: What is Microsoft Teams? Why are we using Microsoft Teams, or why should we? How is Microsoft Teams different from all the other options we have now? Who should be using Microsoft Teams? When is the right time to move away from email or a phone call and work in Microsoft Teams? How should our team set up our Team (or Teams) in Microsoft Teams to improve teamwork and connect with other teams in their Teams across our organisation's team of teams (and their Teams) in Microsoft Teams? *sigh*

As you may soon experience, talking about Microsoft Teams and the different permutations of teams and teamwork can sometimes be overwhelming and confusing (we can blame the Microsoft Teams naming team for that).

In most organisations, there are a handful of people that can navigate that overwhelm and understand the true potential of the new ways of working that Microsoft Teams creates. Generally, most people just want to get their job done and don't have the time to figure out "yet another thing that the IT team has thrown at us." Many of your direct reports may be thinking, "just tell me what I have to do, and I will do it!"

We have seen it in the faces of the customers we have worked with since Microsoft Teams originally launched in March 2017: no matter what industry we work with, no matter the seniority of the staff, a few people just "get it". They jump right in, set up one, or four or twenty-nine different Teams. They add different channels to help structure or filter the different topics the team is focused on. Then, they invite everyone in to participate.

The problem is that those who "get it" assume a lot of knowledge that the rest of the team don't have yet. The rest of the team understands that this could be a better way of working…but they're not quite sure where to start.

The purpose of this book is to help you—the influential executive, the rising star manager, the early career team leader, or the one person in your team that really wants to improve the way "we have always done things"—to bring new ways of working to life, with Microsoft Teams.

It doesn't matter that you haven't used Microsoft Teams yet, or if you have given it a shot and created a few Teams for yourself. This book isn't really about Microsoft Teams and force-feeding you how to use its functionality. Instead, this book focuses on helping you and your team to improve a business process or a work practice that you engage in every day, empowered by Microsoft Teams, by giving you a framework to think about how you design the style of the communication, collaboration, and coordination space for your team (however you define team).

The business process or work practice you seek to improve could be how you run your weekly team meeting.

It could be how you conduct stakeholder engagement across (or outside of) your organisation. It could be how you bring together project teams or virtual teams to make things happen. It could be how you build your annual report or how you manage your recruitment process. The possibilities for business improvement powered by Microsoft Teams are immense. Navigating your way to unlocking that value can be frustrating. This book aims to make it as easy as possible for you, and, in the process, to help you look like the people-first, digitally-enabled, customer-orientated, and cost-conscious manager that you know you are...and your peers want to be!

How to Make the Most of This Book

We have structured this book in three parts. For those of you who are new to Microsoft Teams—who want to build an understanding of what Microsoft Teams is and, more importantly, understand how you can use it as an executive, manager, or team leader—start with Part One. The three chapters in Part One focus on introducing Microsoft Teams through the lens of the three activities we all do as managers: we communicate, we collaborate and we coordinate. Improve those skills as a manager, and you improve your ability to coach and lead your team to success. In each chapter of Part One, we focus on one of the communication, collaboration and coordination management skills and introduce how the capability you have available at your fingertips in Microsoft Teams can help improve your impact in your role.

In Part Two, we tighten our focus onto two of those management skills: collaboration and coordination. We introduce a framework you can use—the 10Ps of Microsoft Teams Design—to help you create the perfect Microsoft Teams powered workspace (or workspaces). The business-led approach of the 10Ps framework will ensure that you don't just recreate the problems you have today: trying to manage your overflowing inbox and chasing status updates from your direct reports. Instead, the 10Ps will ensure you and your team can focus on the right work at the right time, understand how best to work with each other, and ultimately empower your team to achieve more.

Armed with the 10Ps framework, you will be well on your way to Microsoft Teams success. In Part Three, we illustrate what success can look like through patterns that can be seen in how managers around the world are using Microsoft Teams to improve both simple and complex work processes. These patterns are presented using the 10Ps framework, enabling you to see them in practice. Part Three will provide you with the inspiration you need—to simply copy a use case to implement for your team or to help you spark the creation of a new and novel approach to solving a real business problem.

If you are new to Microsoft Teams or have limited experience with tools like Skype for Business, Lync, SharePoint or Planner, we recommend you start with Part One. This will give you the foundation you need to understand how you could use Microsoft Teams today. If you are familiar with Microsoft Teams and are a member or owner of a few Teams already, Parts Two and Three are where you should focus your attention. Some of our beta readers found that starting with the examples and use cases in Part Three helped them understand what is really possible, whereas others enjoyed starting with the simplicity of the 10Ps framework to help them come to grips with how they could better structure the Teams they already engage in. Either way, we encourage you to choose your own adventure through the book to ensure you can unlock value as soon as possible.

Make the Leap to Microsoft Teams

You might be asking yourself: is it worth going through the pain of changing how we do things now and making the leap to improved ways of working with Microsoft Teams? We think so! It doesn't matter if your team is out in the field cutting sugar cane, in a laboratory doing research, planning a product launch, teaching a course with 1500 students at a university, entering new markets or managing the financials of a multi-national organisation—there will be a variety of simple and increasingly complex ways by which your work today could be improved using Microsoft Teams.

Microsoft Teams can't and won't solve everything (despite what the marketing folk and some IT teams will tell you), but it can help you as a manger to reduce the overwhelm of your team, increase your situational awareness, and create the opportunity for work to be front and centre rather than diluted across multiple silos. This will help you empower your people to do more.

We might be biased, but to highlight the power of Microsoft Teams, we wrote this entire book using Microsoft Teams., from the initial sketches and notetaking as we planned the structure of the book (in the Team's shared OneNote notebook), to multiple authors engaging in many conversations while working on one manuscript (co-authored in the "working manuscript" channel). We invited our two external book writing coaches into our workspace to share our work and help make the book a reality. Our beta readers shared their feedback with us by "emailing" the beta reader channel, so all the feedback was captured in one spot. The surveys the beta readers filled out using Microsoft Forms were added as "tabs" to that channel, so the authors could all see the feedback in real time. Then, finally, the planning and execution of the book launch with our marketing agency was conducted in Microsoft Teams. Communication, collaboration and coordination in action.

Now is the time for you to write the next chapter in your story. It's time to explore how you can amplify your impact as an executive, manager or team leader using Microsoft Teams.

BEFORE WE BEGIN

As you may have noticed during the introductory chapter, talking about Microsoft Teams (and the Team you create for your team) can quickly become confusing.

To help you differentiate between these commonly used terms in this book, we have purposely used different capitalisation. Here is a quick guide that will help you understand what we are talking about.

- **Microsoft Teams**: the software that your IT team has installed on your work computer or loaded onto your phone/tablet

- **Team**: a "collaboration and coordination" space that you can create using Microsoft Teams

- **team**: the group of people that report to you/the team that you are a member of in the real world.

When in doubt, if the word starts with a capital letter, we are referring to the product or a feature of the product. If it starts with a lower-case letter, we are referring to what you are familiar with in the real world.

What About "Desktop, vs Browser, vs Mobile"?

One of the great things about Microsoft Teams is that you can have a similar experience regardless of the device you use. Throughout the book, we will flip-flop between referring to the Microsoft Teams app installed on your PC or Mac and the Microsoft Teams app installed on your phone, iPad, or tablet. We will not mention the browser often, but remember that you can access Microsoft Teams via the Office 365 portal if you ever need to.

Now that we have mentioned the mobile app, this begs the question: "Should I install the Microsoft Teams app on my phone?" If you already have your work email on your device and plan to put some or all of this book into practice, then adding the Microsoft Teams app to your phone will help you get things done. We are conscious, however, that many people reading this may still want to maintain some separation between work and their non-work lives.

For those worried that installing the Microsoft Teams app on their phone may start blurring the boundaries, we recommend you become familiar with the "Quiet Hours" feature of Microsoft Teams, which will mute all notifications outside of the core hours you set. It's the perfect blend of convenience in your pocket, with control for blocking potential distractions from your evenings or weekends with family or friends.

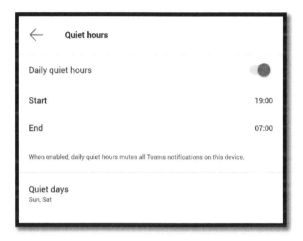

End of Chapter Checklist

○ Download the Microsoft Teams app onto your phone (it is free to download)
○ Turn on the Quiet Hours feature to suit your personal needs.

PART ONE

GETTING TO KNOW MICROSOFT TEAMS

Your IT team has just rolled out Microsoft Teams. If the project team rolling out Microsoft Teams has done a great job, at this stage you should know what Microsoft Teams is and how you could start using it to improve the way you work with your colleagues and direct reports. In the rare case where the project team has only focused on turning the technology on, you might be asking yourself, "What is Microsoft Teams, and what is in it for me?"

In this part of the book, we will make sure that you have a clear understanding of what Microsoft Teams is. Instead of listing hundreds of features that will overwhelm most people, we have structured this section into three chapters. Each chapter is focused on an activity that all executives, managers, and team leaders do every day:

- Communicating
- Collaborating
- Coordinating.

We will walk through each of those activities and show you how the capability within Microsoft Teams can help you do just that. While you may have used Skype for Business or Lync, SharePoint or Planner in the past, we still recommend you read all three chapters in this part. This will refresh your knowledge of what is possible and improve your practice in a Microsoft Teams world.

When reading the following chapters, note that some of the capability discussed may not be available to you. For example, in many organisations with Microsoft Teams, you will not be able to use it as a replacement for your desk phone with your direct dial-in phone number. This will likely be due to decisions made by your technology team with their business stakeholder representatives regarding the role that Microsoft Teams plays in the overall IT architecture of your organisation. Or, you may be working for the United States government or United States Department of Defense, where features of your Office 365 environment are restricted to meet strict security and compliance standards. As we can't predict how Microsoft Teams has been configured in your organisation, we have presented what Microsoft Teams is capable of *if* everything is turned on. If you see something in the following chapters that you don't see in your Microsoft Teams environment that you feel would help you and your team achieve more, make sure you discuss the possibilities with your management team or Chief Information Officer/IT Manager.

Finally, if you want to dive deeper into any of the capabilities of Microsoft Teams that we share in the following chapters, check out the free training that Microsoft provides online at https://aka.ms/TeamsEndUserTraining.

A DIFFERENT WAY TO COMMUNICATE

Email. It's the de facto standard of office communication for knowledge workers, and the lifeblood of commerce and customer service in organisations around the world. It's also the one thing that either overwhelms or controls the workday of almost everyone in your team, your department, and your organisation.

While email has served many people and many organisations well, and will continue to do so into the future, there are aspects of our email culture which get in the way of getting work done. Many people consider whatever is at the top of their inbox as the next item on their to-do list, resulting in their priorities being set by others rather than themselves or their manager. Others religiously check their inbox every 15 minutes so they don't miss important content…but in the process get distracted by the noise created by emails that are not relevant to them, the task at hand, or their role. In fact, email has become so entrenched that many organisations (mostly before making the move to Office 365) send people home if the email server goes down.

Email, just like the love letters your grandparents wrote to each other, or messages in bottles thrown into the water to float around the world, is a way to communicate with someone *with a longer feedback loop*: when you don't need a response straight away. You craft your thoughts, put them into a digital format, add a subject that (ideally) helps the reader understand the purpose of the message, add your intended recipient or recipients, and hit send. You then switch to the next task on your to-do list (or next email to reply to) until you receive a response.

Despite email being a tool for longer feedback loops, we have started to use it when we need a shorter feedback loop as well, where we expect a response in real time, or as close as possible. As pressure has increased for us to be more agile, more responsive, to achieve and exceed our service level expectations or simply get on top of things, email has remained the "catch-all" communication tool we use to try and do it all.

The result? Our inboxes are consistently overflowing. We need to consistently monitor them to respond to the short feedback loop communications coming in. And we are consistently drawn away from doing the work we need to do.

If you spend most of your day getting to "inbox zero" but not getting your work done, are overwhelmed by the 50-200+ new emails you get every day, or simply want to add some nuance to how you communicate with your team, Microsoft Teams provides capability—if used well—to help you feel more in control, support your team to achieve more, and to help you achieve your KPIs. In this chapter, let's explore how the tools you have at your fingertips within Microsoft Teams—presence, chat messages, audio and video calling, simple meetings, and screen sharing—can augment or replace your reliance on email.

Getting a Quick Response—Chat and Presence

Situation: You need a quick response from a colleague to help you solve a problem that is in front of you now.

To reach out to a team member or colleague for advice to navigate a challenge ahead of you, the first thing we are going to do is to initiate a chat with them.

If it is the first time you have tried to connect with this person via chat in Microsoft Teams:

1. Click on the chat button on the left-hand side of Microsoft Teams
2. Start a new chat by clicking on the "square with a pencil" icon at the top of your chat list
3. Type the name of the person or people you want to chat with in the To: line
4. Type your message into the "type a new message box" and hit send (enter, or the paper plane icon).

If you have chatted with this person recently, then simply go to your recent chat list. You will notice—unlike Skype for Business or Lync previously—Microsoft Teams has *persistent* chat. This means that you can always see the history of the chats/requests/advice you have shared with that individual or small group. There is less need to keep an email trail as a back-up, and you can share the history of the chat with others as they join the conversation.

One other consideration, especially if you need a quick response, is to understand whether that person is available and in a position to assist. You can use the presence or availability indicators in Microsoft Teams to understand if that person is able to help. Simply look at the picture or icon of the person you wish to communicate with in the chat window or the recent chat list. The presence indicator is the little circle, and the colours mean the following:

- Green—available
- Yellow with clock hands—away
- Red—busy or in a meeting
- Dark red with a white horizontal line—do not disturb, or currently presenting their screen to others
- Purple circle with an arrow—out of office
- Grey circle with an x in the middle of it—presence cannot be determined.

Ultimately, at its core, the chat experience within Microsoft Teams is quite like the chat experiences you have in your personal life, using apps like WhatsApp, iMessage or Messenger. Like those tools, you can use the built-in camera or image gallery on your phone or tablet to share photos or screenshots with others. By simply taking a photo of a situation, asset or event and posting it in a chat to one of your team, you can eliminate a lot of miscommunication and solve problems quickly. When taking a photo within the Microsoft Teams app on your phone, you can quickly use your finger to draw on or mark up the image before you send it. This is perfect for adding arrows, question marks or other visual guides you need for communicating meaning in your message.

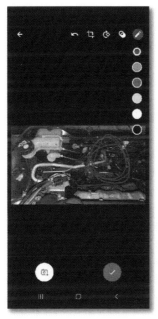

One of the built-in security features of Microsoft Teams means that if you are taking images using the camera within the Microsoft Teams app, the image is not stored locally on the phone or tablet. This ensures that potentially sensitive customer, patient or student information is not left unprotected on a team member's personal device.

Finally, sometimes you may need to send a message or an image to a colleague but also tell them where you are. The Microsoft Teams app gives you the ability to use the built-in GPS in your phone to pin your location on a map and send it in the chat window. This is perfect if you have team members out in the field and they need you to know their location for safety or other reasons.

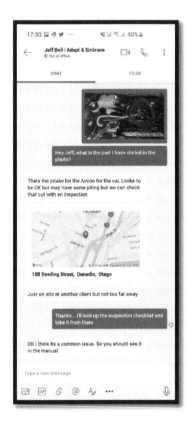

Adding Richness to the Conversation — Audio and Video

Situation: You want to hear the voice or see the body language of the person on the other end of the line.

While a lot of meaning can be communicated through text, your tone of voice and body language can enhance communication and improve comprehension.

There are some corporate myths as to how much communication relies on body language or tone of voice. The most famous is Albert Mehrabian's seven% rule. In 1971, Mehrabian suggested that the credibility of a message is based on body language (to a degree of 55%), and on tone of voice (38%). The remaining 7% is the content of the message (Mehrabian, 1971). The original study only looked at single words, like "maybe," and not flowing conversations or speeches. Well thought out, well-structured text has a far greater impact—just think of any book, article, website, or report you have read recently. So, if a message can still be communicated well via text, why do we need to add richness to our conversation using audio or video? It is a matter of trust.

Studies have demonstrated that well-structured communication with video turned on can achieve the same levels of trust between participants as face-to-face communication, albeit a little bit more slowly. This is particularly important if you are managing or working with distributed teams where you may not have the opportunity to meet face-to-face every week, month or year. At *Adopt & Embrace*, we live and breathe this every day. As a distributed team, we almost never talk to each other on the phone. Instead, we use video calls within Microsoft Teams to ensure we have face-to-face conversations with each other, irrespective of geography.

For example, John, one of the Adoption Specialists in our team, lives in Perth. Perth has a population of just over 2 million people and is situated on the west coast of Australia. It is one of the most isolated major cities in the world. The closest city with a population of over 100,000 people is Adelaide, which is over 2,100 kilometres (or 1,305 miles) away. John meets with us in person once or twice a year. However, at least three or four times a week, he is on a video call either individually or with the team. That isolation completely disappears when you use video to communicate, so much so that when we do meet in person, it feels exactly the same as talking to someone you sit next to in the office every day. Using video helps us not only to remain connected as a distributed team but also to access skills and expertise from around the world.

Adding audio or video to your text-based chat is simple. Look to the top right-hand corner of the chat window you have open and click on the "phone" if you want to have an audio call or the "camera" if you want to have a video call. Don't worry too much if you click the wrong button, you can switch between the two by turning your camera off and on during your conversation. Many people try video for the first time in a high-pressure situation like a meeting. Take the pressure off yourself and try a video call with someone in your team, away from the eyes of your peers at the boardroom or meeting table. Set yourself up for success, (especially in an open plan office) with a USB headset to ensure the audio sounds great.

Before we move on, as we are talking about video calling or video conferencing, it is worth talking about two elephants in the room.

- Why would we use video conferencing in Microsoft Teams when we have a perfectly good video conferencing system in our boardroom/meeting room…that no one really uses today?
- Most of our team are uncomfortable or just don't like using video conferencing as they are worried that they may look funny/strange/different on camera (or just don't like the look of their own face).

Let's start with the first one. In most larger businesses, you will have some video conferencing equipment, almost always in your established meeting rooms. The challenge for many organisations is that these meetings rooms are used not only for video conferences but also for normal, non-video-based meetings as well. This results in rooms being booked up and unavailable when you need to use the video conferencing equipment.

The beauty of a video call in Microsoft Teams is that you don't need to book a room at your end and a room at the other end. You can use the webcam built into your laptop, your phone, your Surface or your iPad, and have a more engaging conversation with others from the comfort of your desk, office or home. For those in organisations that are thinking of upgrading their meeting rooms or rolling out more video conferencing equipment in the future, there are room-based video conferencing solutions built to work seamlessly with Microsoft Teams. Win/Win.

This is especially true if you use some of the meeting room capabilities like Microsoft Teams Rooms Content Camera. This technology (which we can only describe as magic) recognises the physical whiteboard in your room and converts what you are drawing on the board into digital ink (even that green whiteboard marker that never seems to really work). In the process, the person in front of the whiteboard becomes transparent, allowing you to see the entire whiteboard in the meeting.

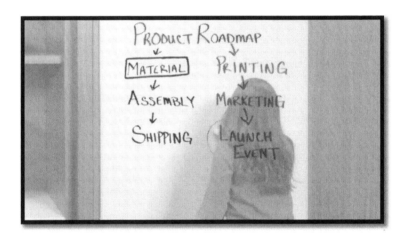

Even without the content camera, you can take a photo of your physical whiteboard and upload it into your meeting, switching from physical ink to digital ink in a matter of seconds.

To cut a long story short, having video conferencing capability at your fingertips (and not locked away in a room that is always booked) improves your workforce's ability to access the technology, increase its usage, and ultimately increase the value of video conferencing in your organisation.

Now, onto the second elephant in the room. What about people who hate having their camera turned on? This is a tougher nut to crack, as this may be up there with some of the greatest fears that many people have: public speaking, swimming with sharks, having my webcam turned on! Despite the fact that we see Sharon, Kevin, Amanda or Daniel's face every day when we talk to them in the office, the act of turning on a webcam so "others can see me" can bring out a lot of anxiety and a lot of excuses. "My hair is a mess today"; "I am working from home, and it won't look professional"; "No one needs to see me, I have a face for radio." All may be valid excuses (yes, Daniel, you do have a face for radio); however, there are ways to slowly convince your colleagues that turning their video camera on is more beneficial not only for them but also for the team.

The normal pattern of success we see is for one brave person to make the first move. If you are reading this book right now, I have volunteered you to be that brave person! Next time you get on a call, turn it into a video call or add your camera to the audio call you are having. Don't ask the other person to turn their camera on. Start your conversation as if it were a regular call. One of two things will happen. The person on the other end may turn video on as well. PERFECT! A habit is starting to be formed. If not, don't worry. Wait until your next call and turn your camera on. This time, halfway through the call, casually say "hey, I can't see you, is your webcam turned on?" That will cause the person on the other end to either apologise and turn their camera on quickly or start rolling out an excuse about hair/makeup/unprofessional background/kids are at home/internet is bad/I am still in my pyjamas. Don't pressure them into turning video on unless they are comfortable. That comfort will come as you engage with them more and more with your video turned on.

It can be easier to convince others to turn their video on if you agree as a group that it is a good idea, prior to getting on calls. Suggest that "it would be great as a team that we all agree that we are going to turn our video on, which in turn will help us reduce an hour-long commute to the office each week for a face-to-face discussion." Or, "if we chat using video, it will stop us from having to find the time to go to the meeting room up on level seven." This will make it easier to start having these richer digital conversations.

Finally, if all else fails, you can use technology to help some of those "excuses" go away. While we don't have the ability for Microsoft Teams to do our hair yet (although the way that augmented reality is going, picking your haircut for a business video call must be just around the corner), there are ways to create a video experience that is more inclusive and accessible. The "background blur" feature of a Microsoft Teams video call is perfect to use when you are working from home and want to hide the pile of ironing you have sitting in the corner of your office (true story), or the mess that your nine-year-old kids have made on the floor (also a true story). Background blur is another technology I can only describe as magic (others may call it real-time video pattern recognition) that identifies where your face and shoulders are in the frame of the video and then applies a blur to any video that is in the background. With background blur turned on, the people you are communicating with can clearly see you, but the rest of your home office, or the "busyness of the café," is just, well, a blur.

Based on the same technology, Microsoft has added the capability not only to blur but also to entirely replace the background of your video call. Now you can work from the comfort of your home office but make it look like you are at HQ, or working from the beach. Unlike the weatherperson on the evening news, you don't need a green screen to use this feature. Just select the background you want, and Microsoft Teams will do the rest.

For example, here's what it looks like when you go from home office to your actual office with just a couple of clicks:

One of my favourite examples of someone using this technology to solve both problems we have just discussed at the same time is our Microsoft Teams model in the last two photos, Loryan Strant. Loryan is a Microsoft Teams/Microsoft 365 Consultant from Australia who regularly uses the background replacement feature to encourage others to turn their video camera on. He has even created a background image that simply says, "turn your camera on."

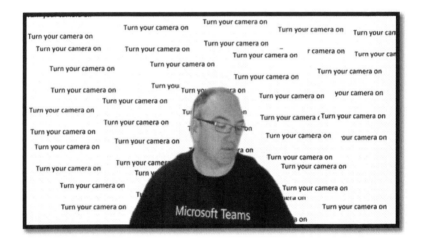

Providing Some Context—File and Screen Sharing

Situation: You want to show someone what you are talking about.

A lot of the time when you are communicating directly with your peers, it may be about a file. Or you may want to share your screen with them so they can see what you see. With Microsoft Teams, it is easy to add this context to your conversation.

Firstly, *you need to stop emailing files to each other*! You know what I am talking about. "Final Report.docx," "Final Report v2.docx," "Final Report v2 PW Edits.docx," "Final Report v2 Final Final.docx." Instead of emailing different versions of the same file back and forth, resulting in the additional overhead required to consolidate all the versions into your final document, share the file in your chat using Microsoft Teams.

The file-sharing capability in a Microsoft Teams chat uses OneDrive for Business—part of your organisations Office 365 subscription—to easily and securely share the file with your peer.

To share a file in your chat, simply click on the "paperclip" button in the chat window. Then, browse for your file on OneDrive or upload the file from your computer. Teams will then organise this to be sent to whomever you are working with.

Note that this is a "link" to the document stored in your OneDrive, not a copy of the document, as it would be if you emailed an attachment to someone.

As the Word document, Excel spreadsheet or PowerPoint presentation is being shared from OneDrive, it means that both of you can work on the *same* document at the *same* time—what Microsoft calls "co-authoring."

Using the co-authoring capability means that you can see each other's changes in real time, reducing the need to send files back and forth.

No more "Final Report v2 Final Final APPROVED.docx."

The added benefit of working on the document, spreadsheet or presentation stored in OneDrive is that you have an automatic version history as well (just in case you make a big mistake and need to go back!).

We will talk more about working with documents, spreadsheets and presentations as a team in the next chapter, where we explore collaboration in more detail.

Being able to quickly show someone what is on your screen can help everyone get on the same page. Whether it is to show one of the support people in your IT team the error message you are getting when you try to raise a purchase order in your finance system, or to walk someone through a document or presentation 1:1, screen-sharing can help reduce misunderstanding or miscommunication and help you achieve the result you desire more quickly.

To share your screen, you need to be in an audio or video call. Click on the "sharing tray" icon in the lower middle of your screen. This will display a few things.

Firstly, you can choose to share your screen in its entirety. If you have multiple monitors, you can select which monitor you want to share. If, however, you have multiple applications open, maybe you don't want the person on the other end to see everything on your screen. In the sharing tray, you can select a specific application. If you select that application, the person on the other end will only see that window. Any other window you have on your desktop will be invisible to them. This means you don't need to close the forty-seven windows you have open before you share your screen or be worried about random chat messages or notifications popping up during your conversation.

Need to Escalate Something?

If you are in conversation and need to find another expert, or escalate your discussion to a manager, you can access your organisation chart within your chat. Simply click on the "Organisation" tab to quickly see who the person you are talking to reports to, and who reports to them.

Communicating at Scale Across Your Organisation

Situation: We have our all-hands meetings over the next two weeks, which means I need to travel to every location.

As an executive or a manager, you may be accountable for communicating at scale. Traditionally, this may be done through an all-staff email. You might have a "CEO connection" group in Yammer where you provide updates to the workforce. Or, it could be through in-person events — your "quarterly update" or "sales kick-off" or "departmental roadshow." If you are part of a large organisation, it may mean getting on a plane (at 5 am) and travelling across the country, or across the world to meet regularly with your teams on the ground.

We are not suggesting that visiting your sites is a bad idea; rather, you can increase your visibility at those sites and in turn enable yourself to have far more productive conversations while on site, by broadcasting your presentation to everyone at once. By live streaming one event to every staff member, you don't have to deliver the same presentation twenty-six times, and you get to spend more time on site having a deeper, more meaningful impact. The presentation can be viewed at people's desks (or in a meeting room), and it can be recorded, transcribed and translated as well...in close to real time.

Broadcasting a presentation to your department, division or organisation is easy with the Live Events capability in Microsoft Teams. While it takes a little bit more than "just turning on our webcam and inviting 5000 people to attend," it is relatively straightforward to set up without any intervention from your IT team. We won't bore you with all the details now; however, Microsoft has put together a great online guide that you or one of your team can work through—https://aka.ms/LiveEvents. Use this guidance to quickly and easily broadcast your next event or all-hands presentation (and avoid the airport at 5 am!).

Moving Away from My Traditional Desk Phone

As moving away from your traditional desk phone requires the most effort from your IT team to set up, we have left it for last. Microsoft Teams can be a replacement for your traditional phone system as well as everything else. Instead of using a desk phone or another system as your soft phone, Microsoft Teams can be configured with your normal landline or direct dial-in number. Anywhere you have an internet connection, you can use Microsoft Teams to both make and receive calls. Many of our customers are planning to move to Microsoft Teams for their phone system to save money and provide more flexibility to their workforce.

In this chapter, we have explored some of the fundamental communication capabilities you have at your fingertips in Microsoft Teams. By leveraging presence, chat, audio, video, file sharing, screen sharing, and live events, you can communicate effectively with individuals, small groups or your entire organisation. As a manager, these capabilities can help you better connect with people every day. Effective teamwork takes more than just communication, though. In the next chapter, we shift our focus to collaboration: the purposeful pursuit of a shared goal by a group of individuals. We will explore how Microsoft Teams can help you improve the situational awareness of your team, help them focus their efforts in the right direction and ultimately work together to achieve more.

End of Chapter Checklist

- o Send your first chat message to a colleague
- o Turn your chat into a video call and have a face-to-face discussion
- o Add a third person to the discussion
- o Share your screen and walk the person on the other end through a document, report, or presentation
- o Try sending your location in a chat message from the Teams app on your mobile phone
- o Visit https://teamsbook.info and click on 'Resources' to watch a video that shows you how.

A DIFFERENT WAY TO COLLABORATE

Clear communication is the lifeblood of a good team. In the previous chapter, we explored how you can use some of the key features of Microsoft Teams to communicate 1:1 with your team members. Using tools like chat, audio, video, file and screen sharing enables you to communicate your intent, listen directly to feedback, or catch up with one of your direct reports about their weekend.

This chapter builds on the first by starting to explore how we can bring a team together to collaborate using Microsoft Teams.

At present, your team collaborates using a variety of methods. The method of choice likely depends on the urgency of the work and the intended audience. When you need to share something with the whole team, you may have sent an email to a "distribution group." A distribution group is an email address that can be used to send an email to a defined list of people—generally a team. Once you add the distribution list address to the email, a subject is added, sometimes carefully worded to get attention, and if urgent it is marked as "high importance." Files are attached and then sent…resulting in twenty-seven copies of the email sitting in twenty-seven inboxes across your organisation, with twenty-seven duplicates of the file. A reply-all chain reaction starts, resulting in multiple versions of files being updated, conflicting comments in different emails, and three forked conversations happening to the side when someone only replied to a subset of the people on the distribution list. Collaboration via email is a nightmare.

The trouble with collaboration via email is that everyone is using it, and, in most cases, misusing it. Important communication is missed amid the many messages arriving in the inbox of your team members. As a manager, you can't be sure when someone has received and read the message. Yet, you may have chosen to use written communication because it can be referred to when an instruction isn't carried out. But, is it any wonder our team members are missing important messages when everything arrives via email? This is even more problematic when email is used for urgent messages when it would be more appropriate to pick up the phone and get on a conference call.

Conference calls can speed up communication across your team and give you the opportunity to check that the message is understood. They can also help to ensure that everyone is on the same page. The downside, however, is that because it is a "synchronous" communication style, everyone needs to make the time to be on the call. If you are using an audio bridge for a conference call, it lacks any capability to show or share documents, spreadsheets or presentations to help focus the conversation. You may have tools that allow you to set up a virtual meeting with your team and share your screen, but they are outside of the flow of your work.

If only we could simplify this and do it all in one place…

A Space for Your Team to Collaborate

So, how do we set ourselves up with a place for our team to collaborate? Let's explore what a Team in Microsoft Teams is.

At its core, a Team is a space that enables you to bring together people, content and systems or tools that you use every day. It's a place where your people can discuss important topics; create, refine and share documents, spreadsheets and presentations, and; draw on data or information from the array of tools you have across your organisation.

Unlike the distributed and disparate mailboxes that your team uses today, which are all silos of your team's knowledge, creating a Team establishes a centralised place where every member can see what is going on: the conversations, the files being worked on and shared, the task lists being maintained, the notes being taken and the meetings taking place. It consolidates what is happening in your team today—across email, network file shares, audio bridges, video conferencing, Kanban boards on your office wall filled with Post-it notes and more—into a single place where you all can improve your situational awareness, efficiency and effectiveness.

A Team can be created as private, where you as the Team owner have complete control over who has access to participate. Alternatively, it can be created as public, allowing people to discover and join the Team as they wish.

Teams can be created for different purposes, including projects, events, processes, committees, communities of practice, bids, managing customer relationships, and many more. In Part Two of this book, we walk through how to identify the right time to create a Team, and the right way to create a Team.

Adding Nuance to How We Work Together

Within each Team, there is another structure that helps manage and refine the way we collaborate—channels. Channels allow you to group or focus the conversations that are occurring into different subjects, topics, projects, customer journey stages…in fact, any way you think would help add structure to the way your team needs to work together.

Within a channel, your team can engage in conversations, share and co-author documents, meet through both scheduled and ad-hoc meetings, and see each other face-to-face through video. Video conversations can also be recorded, which is perfect for capturing training, process walk-throughs, or important meetings and presentations. The recording is added to the conversation in the context of all the other collaborative activity that is taking place.

Let's look at an example of a Team. Say you are a sales manager, and you have a team of eight business development managers across your territory. You also work closely with a marketing team that reports to your organisation's Chief Marketing Officer. The marketers are assisting with some account-based marketing in your high priority accounts. You could set up a Team that is designed to help your BDMs and the marketers work better together and increase revenue. You create a Team called "Southern Territory Sales & Marketing." Within the team, you want to make sure there is focus on your top five accounts in the territory, so you create five channels, each one named after one of those five high priority accounts. You add a sixth channel called "Research and Trends," where the marketers and BDMs share insights and sales collateral which can be used to help create interest or frame a conversation with your prospects.

Let's look at another example. You are a Human Resources Manager, and you need to run a project to update all the position descriptions in your company in order to comply with a new regulation put in place by the government. You create a Team called "PD Renewal Project" and invite your HR business partners and union representatives to participate. You set it up as a private team, as some of the information may be sensitive until all parties agree on what the position descriptions should look like. Within the Team, you create channels to focus your energy (one simply called "Regulation") where you have shared the new legislation and initiated a conversation across the team about how to interpret the new laws that were put in place. Another channel is "Executive PDs," to ensure there is a focus on the 15 members of your senior executive team, whose position descriptions require additional effort, based on the new rules in place. Another few channels are focused on the different role types across the organisation. Finally, a channel called "Rollout" focuses the conversation on how you plan to distribute the new position descriptions and get your employees to sign their new contracts.

Maybe you are a teacher and want to establish a place where you can collaborate with your students. You create a Team for the subject you are teaching, "Grade 10 Maths." You invite all your students on the class roll into the Team. Channels could be set up by topic area, such as Statistics, Algebra, Calculus. Or, they could be set up in accordance with where you are in the term: Week 1, Week 3, Week 7, etc. Within each channel, you share learning resources, provide guidance, and set challenges for the class to complete together.

Finally, you could be the manager of a large engineering field services team. You want to empower them to be more mobile and draw on the expertise of subject matter experts in HQ, as well as on the collective wisdom of the 34 field service reps in your department. You create a Team called "Electrical Field Service Remote Experts." You create channels focused on the common issues or challenges they face when working on transformers across the countryside: "Safety," "Windings," "Insulation," "Cooling," "Relays," and "Other." Your field engineers use the Teams app on their mobile phones to take photos of issues they face, using their finger to draw arrows on the images before they post them to the appropriate channel for advice. Members of the Team answer the question in real time, enabling the field service engineer to continue their work without delay.

Creating, Refining, and Sharing Knowledge

Now that we have channels to focus our energy and attention in the Team, we can apply that focus to create or refine new knowledge. The simplest way to do this is to actively engage in the channel by posting or contributing to the conversation. This "shared stream of consciousness" from your teammates will enable others in your group to discover new perspectives, explore and make connections between ideas, and apply these to solving complex problems.

Beyond simple conversation, your team members can work on more structured artefacts—documents, spreadsheets and presentations in the channel. Instead of emailing around 15 different copies of the same document with everyone's edits, your team can do all work on the exact same document, reducing the need to consolidate the changes at the last minute. A great example of this in action is how we wrote this book. We set up a Team called "Teams Book Factory," and in the Team there is a channel called "Working Manuscript" to focus our discussions around writing the book. In that channel, we created a word document, set the appropriate page size, margins, and styles for the paperback book size we were targeting, and started writing. Almost three months later, the four authors and two editors have all been working on the exact same file.

This doesn't just apply to Word documents. If you have an upcoming management meeting you need to prepare for, or a pitch to a prospective client, you can bring your team together to work on the presentation or build out the financial model together, instead of siloed individual efforts that someone has to consolidate at the last minute.

Taking Action

Sometimes when you work in a group, you need to get the attention of your colleagues. In the real world, you might just say "Hey Brad, look at this," or "Aleisha, have you updated the management report yet?" When we hear our name, we turn around in our swivel chair and pay attention to whomever is speaking to us. In a digital world, it is a little harder to get someone's attention. Within Microsoft Teams, you can get people's attention through a few different methods: mentions, high importance and priority notifications.

When you type the name of someone in your team into a conversation, you will notice that a box appears, listing that person's name. If you click on that name (or hit enter), that person will be "tagged" in your message. When you send the message, they will receive a notification that someone (you) mentioned them in a post. This is handy when you want to make sure that person sees your message. You don't need to just mention an individual, though. You can mention a channel to get the attention of everyone who is showing or following that channel, or you can mention the entire Team.

Adding importance to a message is just like making an email high importance. In Teams, this function will display an exclamation mark beside the channel to let everyone know there is an important message that needs to be read. It will also feature a red border to help draw your audience's attention to what you need to say.

Finally, if you really, really, really (really) need someone's attention (in an emergency, for example), you can use a priority notification. A priority notification will send an alert, not only to the individual(s) you wish to notify, but also to every device that they have Microsoft Teams logged into, every 2 minutes for 20 minutes. This is a powerful way to disrupt someone's day and get their attention.

Before you get all excited and start pinging your colleagues with notifications—whether through a mention or a priority notification—a word of warning: if someone yelled your name all day, every day, the power of using your name to get your attention would diminish very quickly and likely become very annoying. The same can occur in Microsoft Teams. We do not recommend you use these features to tell people that you have replied to their message or posted something to a channel. Save these features for when you really need them.

As a rule, only use a mention when you need someone to act. That will help preserve the power of the notification as the recipient will not be flooded with them. It will also allow the recipients to triage more effectively and focus their attention on priorities throughout their day.

Priority notifications should be saved for real emergencies: when you're trying to page a consultant to provide life-saving surgery in a hospital, when there is a significant safety issue at your site that all members of the Team need to be aware of, or when the beans have run out in the coffee machine.

Bringing the Team Together

Whether your team has daily stand-ups, weekly meetings, or monthly/quarterly all hands, ensuring your team remains connected and on the same page is important. With conversations occurring in a centralised location, your Team's need to spend time in your meetings sharing updates on what has been happening should reduce, enabling you to spend more time on making decisions, coaching or planning for the future.

You can schedule meetings to occur within a channel inside your Team. This allows you to take advantage of some of the great communication capabilities we discussed in the previous chapter, including high-quality video conferencing and screen sharing, all from the comfort of your desktop, laptop, tablet, or phone. You can use Teams to enable your team to connect into your team meeting from anywhere in the world, whether they're at home on their tablet while one of their children is off sick from school, on their phone at a customer site in between meetings with key stakeholders, or on their laptop in your regional office.

At *Adopt & Embrace*, we have several scheduled meetings that occur each week. One example happens on Tuesdays at 12:30 pm AEST, which is our weekly management team meeting. The recurring meeting was scheduled in Teams and it automatically added an appointment to our Outlook calendar. We can join the meeting from the appointment in Outlook, or simply open Teams and click "Join." As a rule, we have all agreed to turning on our webcams whenever we meet, so we are instantly greeted with the familiar faces of the team across Australia and New Zealand. We use a third-party online tool to manage our company scorecard, issues, and actions, and the meeting facilitator shares her screen so everyone can see what we are discussing that day. We recognise that, occasionally, some members of the team won't be able to make the call because they are stuck in other meetings. Not a problem! We click "Start Recording" to capture the conversation over the next 90 minutes. Once the meeting is done, we stop recording and exit the meeting. Within seconds, the recording of the meeting is added to the conversation in the channel, allowing us to continue the conversation from the meeting through text-based replies and also allowing those that missed the meeting to catch up on the key discussions and decisions of the day.

End of Chapter Checklist

o Think about the time-consuming collaboration processes in your team and note them down.
o Note beside each process how Microsoft Teams capability could help you improve those processes
o Visit https://teamsbook.info and click on "Resources" to watch a video that shows you how this is done.

A DIFFERENT WAY TO COORDINATE

If you are a manager like me, a significant part of a day is spent coordinating. Coordination can mean many things to many people: planning, organising, directing, controlling, scheduling, staffing, reporting…and, in most cases (especially if you're a manager), trying to keep on top of things. Coordination in practice is a mash-up of sourcing information from multiple sources, analysing or synthesising data, making informed decisions and communicating outcomes.

For you, team coordination might mean setting your weekly or monthly roster or staff schedule. Or , it could mean creating your budget for the next 12 months. It could involve putting together your monthly management report, drawing on three different systems of records, or distributing and levelling tasks across your team. It could simply involve running your weekly team meeting and tracking actions off the back of your discussions. No matter how you coordinate today, I am reasonably confident that a fair amount of your coordination occurs via email. Maybe you draw on reports that get emailed to you every night, or you email the roster to your whole Team every fortnight.

Coordinating Your Team Tasks and Actions

By adding a "Planner" tab to a channel, you can visually track the tasks or actions that your team are currently working on. If you currently use Post-it notes on a wall, or like the simplicity of visual task management that a Kanban board provides, you can have a similar experience within Microsoft Teams. In Teams, you can have a single plan for your team, or, if you're managing a lot of complexity, break it up into multiple plans aligned to the channels in your Team.

First, you need to add the Planner tab to your channel. Click on the "+" new tab button to the right of "Conversations" and "Files" at the top of your screen, then select "Planner" from the apps that appear in the "Add a tab" box. Create a new plan and give your tab a suitable name.

There is a simple structure to a plan created in Planner: tasks and buckets. Tasks have a name and due date and can be assigned to someone. To add a task, simply type in a task name and click "add task." To help speed up the job of adding tasks to your plan, you can add all your tasks before setting due dates or assigning to individuals. If you have more than a handful of tasks, it makes sense to group them into different buckets. The buckets in your plan are the same as the columns you might have on your wall to group your Post-it notes together. To add a bucket, simply click the "Add new bucket" button and give your bucket a name. Once you have created a bucket, you can drag and drop your tasks into the different buckets.

If you are a member of multiple Teams that are using Planner, and you also need to manage your own personal to-do list, it can become overwhelming. Microsoft Teams makes it easy to see all your assigned tasks in one place: the "Tasks" app, which you can find on the left-hand side of the Teams application, or on your mobile phone.

Many managers we work with are already using tools to manage the tasks of their team. Maybe you are using Asana, Trello, Smartsheet, or others. The good news is, if you like using those tools, you can keep using those tools. Phew! Instead of adding a "Planner" tab to your channel, you can use the "Asana," "Trello," or "Smartsheet" tabs and link directly to the project, board, or sheet relevant to your work. If you use an online tool that doesn't have a built-in tab, as long as the website you access starts with "https://," you can use the "Website" tab to deep link directly to the relevant page or view in that tool.

At *Adopt & Embrace*, we use the "Website" tab to do just that: provide easy access to the specific project plans, budgets, and actual figures inside Avaza, our SaaS project management tool, directly inside each customer-focused Team.

Other tabs can help you provide the right information to your team, enabling them to make the right decisions. For example, if you have developed dashboards using Power BI, you can use the "Power BI" tab to enable your team to quickly refer to metrics and key performance indicators without the need to go searching for that report in another browser window.

Coordinating Your Staff

Within Microsoft Teams, you can create and manage a schedule for your team, using the "Shifts" app. While this capability is designed for "first-line" workforces, like those in retail, healthcare, hospitality, field service, or customer service… It can also be useful for more traditional white-collar roles where you need to coordinate people across specific timeframes. For example, you may need to plan the annual leave for your team (our favourite use case!), staff a booth at a tradeshow you are sponsoring, or manage who from your team is on call for any inbound requests or escalations.

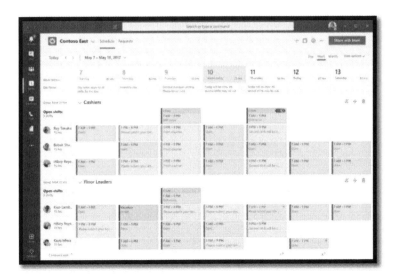

To create a schedule, simply click on the "Shifts" app on the left-hand side of your Microsoft Teams window. It will likely be hidden behind the ellipsis button (the three dots).

Once you are in the Shifts app, you first need to create a schedule. Schedules are based on Teams, so if you already have an existing Team for the group you wish to coordinate, select that Team when the "Choose a team schedule to create" dialog box appears. Then, set a time zone for this team.

Once your schedule has been created, you can add and assign shifts to your team members. A "shift" has a date, start and end time, a custom label (if you want to give your shift a name), and the ability to add specific activities that the team member should do during the shift. For example, you could add the lunch break, when you want them to be on the front counter, or when you want them to be working in the stock room.

Once you have assigned your shifts, the last step you need to do is to publish the schedule to your team. Once published, your team will get notifications via the Microsoft Teams app on their mobile phone about what shifts they have been assigned for that week.

If you are not ready to assign shifts to specific team members, or you want to give your team a choice of shifts, you can create an "open shift." An open shift is one that has not yet been assigned to an employee and could be requested by a team member once the schedule has been published. As the manager, when your team requests open shifts, you can approve or deny those requests. The approval request provides you with additional information to help you make an informed decision, for example, whether it would conflict with a current shift that team member has been assigned to or the number of hours the individual has been assigned in the schedule already.

If you want to track the actual time that your team is spending on a shift, you can leverage the Time Clock. Time Clock is accessed via the Microsoft Teams mobile app and enables your team to "clock on" and "clock off" their shift. The Time Clock can also use the GPS or location on the team members' phones to help you understand where they are clocking on and off shift—whether in your store, at an event or off site. All the shift data can be exported using an Excel spreadsheet so you can reconcile it against your team or event budget.

Finally, you can use the shifts app as a simple way for your team to request time off, such as parental leave, vacation or sick days. In this app, your team member requests the leave, and you can approve, deny, or ask them for additional information. Once approved, the requested time off appears in the schedule.

Coordinating Your Response

If you manage a customer service team, there are likely systems you rely on to notify you of incoming jobs, tasks or issues that need your attention. Today, this may arrive via an email alert into an individual or shared mailbox. In your Team, instead of relying on forwards and reply-all emails to coordinate a response, you can push those alerts into dedicated channels. By simply replying to the alert, your team can craft their response and put their plan into action.

There are a few different ways to send your alerts from third-party systems into Microsoft Teams. Firstly, you can simply divert your alerts away from your shared mailbox and directly into a channel in your Team. Each channel has its own email address, so you can simply click on the ellipsis (the three dots) beside the channel name and select "Get Email Address." Anything sent to this address will appear as a message in that channel.

If you use a customer service or interaction tool like Intercom, Zendesk, UserVoice or others, there are built-in "connectors" you can set up for your channel. Each connector plugs into your third-party system and, once configured, will send alerts from those tools into your channel. This is perfect if you want a notification whenever a new ticket is raised.

Finally, if you are serious about streamlining both your notifications and how you respond to them, you can use Power Automate (previously known as Flow) to refine and perfect processes for your team. Power Automate provides you with the ability to define workflow logic. For example: for any alert above priority level 500, send to channel x. For any alert above priority level 1000, include a high importance tag on the post. Above level 1500, send an SMS to the phone of the CEO.

Not sure where to start? There are plenty of examples and templates available that you can build on from the Microsoft Power Automate homepage at https://powerautomate.microsoft.com.

Now that we have explored how managers can use Microsoft Teams to communicate, collaborate and coordinate, one question remains. How do we best establish our Team (or Teams) to set ourselves up for success? How do we ensure that we can effectively collaborate and coordinate with each other? How many Teams should I create? What channels should we use? How do I ensure all our participants are on the same page?

In the next part of the book, we consider how best to design and structure work in Microsoft Teams to help you achieve both your professional and personal goals.

End of Chapter Checklist

o   Think about the time-consuming coordination processes in your team and note them down.
o   Note beside each process how Microsoft Teams capability could help you improve those processes
o   Visit   https://teamsbook.info   and   click   on "Resources" to watch a video that shows you how this is done.

PART TWO

THE 10PS:

A FRAMEWORK FOR COLLABORATION AND COORDINATION SUCCESS

In Part One, we explored how Microsoft Teams can help executives, managers and team leaders to better communicate, collaborate and coordinate. You are now equipped with the knowledge you need to engage effectively in targeted communication with your team members, your boss and other stakeholders across your organisation. However, the collaboration and coordination possibilities may be overwhelming you now.

You may be asking yourself: what is the right way to set up a collaboration space for my team/project/department? How do I get my team on board? Do I just create a Team for my team and tell them to stop emailing each other? Is it better to have one Team with lots of channels, or a handful of Teams with fewer channels? What should I call my team? What if I want external customers or suppliers to participate? What happens to the Team once this project is finished?

Ever since we started working with customers to help them understand how they can improve business processes and work practices with Microsoft Teams, we have heard those questions and many more, time and time again. Soon, we realised that we were answering those questions in an increasingly consistent way. The result? The 10Ps framework for Microsoft Teams Design:

- Problem
- Purpose
- People
- Priorities
- Principles
- Plugins
- Permissions
- Performance
- Provisioning
- Perishability.

In the following chapters, we will explore each "P" in the 10Ps framework. Together, they will help you ideate, establish and configure spaces where you and your colleagues can effectively collaborate on and coordinate your work. The decisions you make based on each of the 10Ps will help you refine the way you use Microsoft Teams, resulting in:

- Better situational awareness

- Increased ability to focus
- Reduced risk of sharing information with those who shouldn't have access to it
- Reduced overwhelm from too many meaningless notifications
- A structured way to communicate to your peers how you are using Teams.

PROBLEM

Think about the last time you made a change in your life. Maybe it was a simple tweak, like taking a different route home on your daily commute. Maybe the change was something a little bit more significant and you decided to lose some weight to get back in shape. Maybe you refinanced your home loan or mortgage with another bank at a better interest rate.

Whatever the change you made, I am almost certain that you would not have made it if it were not for one thing: recognising that you had a problem in the first place.

"There was a traffic jam up ahead," is a problem. "I am carrying more weight than I should, which is impacting my heart," is a problem. "We are struggling to keep up with our house payments," is a problem.

Problems are great to have when you seek to make a change in your personal life, as they can provide context for yourself and the people around you as to why the changes you are about to make are important. However, the power of problems doesn't just apply in your personal life. Problems can be great in a professional context as well, especially if you are trying to persuade people around you—your team, committee or project group—to embrace new behaviours at work. You might be familiar with the principle of the "golden circle" made famous by Simon

Sinek's TEDx talk "How great leaders inspire action" (Sinek, 2009) and his book, *Start With Why* (Sinek, 2011).

Don't Just Say, "Let's Start Using Teams"

Sure, you could just tell everyone, "We are using Microsoft Teams now—so stop emailing and start posting messages in the 'Marketing team' Team I just created." And some of your team would start to switch some of their work over into the collaboration space you created.

Our experience shows that, when introduced in this manner, the level of engagement in a Team is generally short-lived. People don't understand why they need to make the change. You will have a situation where around one-third of your team are in Microsoft Teams, while the rest are still hanging on for dear life to the email filing system they have perfected during 25 years in the workforce. Maybe it is the "simplicity" of the 12-level deep file hierarchy they have created on the network drive. When there are pre-existing, entrenched ways of doing things in your team, a switch to Microsoft Teams dictated by the manager isn't sustainable in the long term. A lot of "unlearning" needs to take place.

The result of just jumping in may well be a Team that starts with a flurry of activity, then dies a slow death as individuals switch back to how they used to do things with email and that file hierarchy in the shared drive.

So, how do we ensure that we set ourselves up for success and increase the likelihood that our team comes with us on our Microsoft Teams journey? There are two dimensions to "Problem", the first of the 10Ps, that we need to consider.

Firstly, does your team understand what problems they are solving when they change their style of collaboration and coordination to one that flourishes in Microsoft Teams?

Secondly, is it clear what real problems are being solved through collaboration and coordination activity in Microsoft Teams?

The former ensures that your team understands why they are switching a lot of what they do over to Microsoft Teams. The latter ensures that they are starting to structure the collaboration and coordination spaces that are created in Microsoft Teams in the most efficient and effective way. We will explore both dimensions in this chapter.

The Problem with Collaboration and Coordination

If you have worked for more than about three minutes in almost any organisation in the world, I am sure you have witnessed one of the most insidious features of the modern workplace. You may have been the victim of one yourself: the "reply-all" email thread.

It usually starts out innocently. Christine sends an email to some of her colleagues. "Hi everyone. Here is the first draft of our presentation for the event next Wednesday. What do you think?" A PowerPoint presentation, "Event Presentation.pptx," is attached to the email. Then reality sets in. There are 27 people on the To: line and four on the CC: line. We can't be sure, but there is likely someone BCC'd in as well, just so they have visibility of the first draft. Every one of those individuals has a copy of the email...and a copy of the PowerPoint presentation. You know what happens next: a nightmare which will no doubt fill up your inbox over the next 24 hours.

Within four minutes, the first reply-all email comes in. "Hey Christine, great work. I just made a few minor amendments on your PowerPoint deck, see attached." There is a file now called "Event Presentation-Edits.pptx." Thirty seconds later, Dave shoots his feedback through "Christine—not quite sure about slide 3, can you delete it and replace it with that slide we used for the pitch last month?" An hour later, without reading Dave's feedback, Sandra chimes in with some minor edits, as well as introducing some new formatting that she copied in from another presentation. Suddenly, the original author of the draft presentation is overwhelmed with emails in their inbox, as well as multiple versions of the presentation with conflicting feedback that now needs to be manually merged into one copy.

Anyone who has been in this situation before knows how tough it is. The only way anyone has ever got past this stage is through pure brute force. Someone steps up, usually the original author, who synthesises all that feedback and content together into one final presentation. This normally happens after hours or at the very last minute, because they have so much else on their plate.

This scenario has played itself out in almost every team in almost every organisation in the world. When you break it down, the inefficiency and ineffectiveness of the process is astounding.

Hundreds, if not thousands of emails are sent, triaged, maybe filed and likely deleted depending on the personal preferences of each recipient. Multiple versions of documents are duplicated across everyone's inboxes in an uncontrolled manner. People who remain in the loop and people who are left out of the loop switch between reply-all and simply replying to messages. And, if valuable knowledge has been shared in the process, it is all locked up in everyone's inboxes, making it very hard for your new starter to discover this information and pick things up next week.

In terms of problems that need to be solved, the problem with inefficient collaboration is one that almost everyone in your team will be familiar with. At a bare minimum, making sure your people understand the rationale of why change is necessary will go a long way to helping reinforce new collaboration behaviours.

Being Clear About a Tangible Business Problem

While reducing inefficient communication, collaboration and coordination behaviours is a great starting point, we don't get paid just to be better at working together. I don't know anyone who has got out of bed and said, "I just can't wait to collaborate more today." We need to be solving real business problems, overcoming challenges, governing important processes or taking on opportunities to further the success of our organisation.

Starting with a problem helps make clear why we are changing our work behaviours. It can also help us to better structure our Teams in Microsoft Teams. When we have a list of clearly defined problems or opportunities that we wish to pursue, a good approach is to start with designing a Team for each problem. Don't try to solve two or three or four problems in the one Team, as it's likely that solving each problem will require different people or have different information needs.

When defining the problem you seek to solve, you should ensure the problem is one that people believe is real. There is no point "making up" why we need to work in this new way. Making sure that the problem is both rational and legitimate will ensure that it's a solid foundation for the way that you group. The scope of the problem should make sense for the level that you're operating at in your organisation. "There are roadblocks caused by our learning management system which stop our students from fully engaging in course content," is a great example of a problem for teachers or course coordinators to solve. "In last year's audit, it was identified that there are not sufficient controls in place to determine the right level of investment in capital works projects. Without visibility and improved governance of investment decisions, we may be liable for action from the regulators," is an example of a problem for your Board of Directors or finance team to solve.

To increase the impact of your problem statement, try to be clear about the impact that the problem is causing or the impact that inaction will have. This will ensure that it serves as a more meaningful "why" for your team and keeps the scope of the problem contained to your Team.

Armed with a clear problem statement, you can now progress to the next step of the 10Ps of Microsoft Teams Design: Purpose.

Key Takeaways

1. Being clear about the problem or problems you are trying to solve helps your team understand why they need to switch to more modern ways of collaboration and coordination
2. Avoid trying to solve multiple problems at once with one Team. Don't be afraid to split a problem into multiple Teams
3. Start your design journey with the problems you are solving. This will help you avoid creating another overflowing inbox for your team to manage
4. Your team will benefit from the ability multiple Teams gives them to filter their attention and focus their energy on the right things at the right time.

End of Chapter Checklist

o If you haven't done so yet, download the 10Ps workbook from https://teamsbook.info/ (click on the "Resources" link)
o Using the workbook, fill in Step 1: Problem.

PURPOSE

How many times a day are you distracted by something like an email, interruption or request?

If you answered "almost all day, every day," you would not be alone. According to the *Workplace Distraction Report* published by Udemy, over 70% of the workforce admit they feel distracted when they are working. 16% said that they are almost always distracted (Udemy Research, 2018). The distractions are not necessarily the problem, though. The larger problem is how long it takes to get back on task or back into the flow of work after a distraction occurs. According to research from the University of California, Irvine, it can take an average of 23 minutes to get back on track (Mark, Gudith, & Klocke, 2008). How long does it take for you or your team members to get their focus back after being distracted?

For me, the wasted time it takes post-distraction to get back on top of my priorities is my number one productivity drain. When I am in flow—energised and laser-focused on the outcome I am trying to achieve—work feels effortless and time moves quickly. However, as soon as I'm distracted, it can take many minutes, if not an hour or more, to get back into the highly productive state.

I am sure you have had similar experiences in your work, where you constantly battle with two somewhat opposing forces: the need to get work done and the need to appear to be responsive to and supportive of others. It is a tightrope that many of us, as team leaders, managers and executives try to balance on, every day. Too much focus on the distractions (no matter how urgent or important they are) and you don't get your work done. Too much focus on getting your work done, and your team may flounder without the support, guidance or reassurance they need from you.

As you shift your work out of one of the most efficient distraction machines ever invented (the email inbox, full of everyone else's priorities) and into Microsoft Teams, how do you ensure that you are not setting yourself up for failure due to consistent distractions and the resultant cost of lost time and effort? How do you structure your Teams in Microsoft Teams to give you more control over how you manage your energy and focus through the workday? Based on our experience with customers who have grappled with this challenge over the past few years, there is one approach we have seen that can reduce the need for team members to be consistently checking and triaging Microsoft Teams every 15 minutes (as they have been with their email inbox for the last 20 years. This approach can also empower your staff to control when they best apply their discretionary efforts and attention throughout the day. The approach is called "purpose-based Teams."

So, what is a purpose-based Team? Instead of creating a team based on your organisational structure, like "Marketing Team" or "Human Resources," where the purpose or "why we are here" rationale isn't obviously clear to people outside of your Team, a purpose-based Team focuses on the outcome we want to achieve with our peers. This involves a shift away from the "email distribution list" mentality (that is almost always aligned to structure) and towards an approach that is more results-orientated.

There are a few (very) obvious examples that come to mind, such as having a Team for each project that you are working on. Projects by nature (should) have a clear purpose, so the members of the project understand what they are working together to achieve. Committees are another good example, where people meet regularly to govern specific processes across your business and understand the role they play in forming that group. Projects and committees only just scratch the surface of the different ways groups of people come together for shared purpose in your organisation.

Generally, the more specific the purpose of the Team, the better. "But that means I will be a member of multiple Teams; won't that make it hard to manage?" Good question. At first, you might feel overwhelmed by being a member of three, or seven, or twenty-seven different Teams. However, the beauty of multiple Teams is that it gives you the opportunity to focus your attention on different "purposes" across your day. It allows you to control your attention and not have it controlled by others. Just because you are a member of eight Teams, it doesn't mean that you must have them open, reading every message and responding to every thought throughout the day. Removing the distraction of a Team is as simple as minimising it (or even hiding it) from your Team list. This granularity shouldn't overwhelm; it should help you focus on the one thing that is important to you at the time. If you have all of your Microsoft Teams activity occurring in one Team, you lose the ability to filter or remove those distractions when necessary.

Because you are already clear on the problems you are trying to solve, your task now is to be very clear about the purpose you are trying to achieve as a group. Solving a single problem may require different groups with different purposes, and that is okay! If this is the case, it makes sense to break the Team you are working on into two or more Teams, to ensure that the right focus can be applied at the right time.

What's in a Name?

The other powerful aspect of purpose-based Teams is that the purpose of the group can be a very clear signal to others in the organisation as to why you are here, what you are doing, and whether someone should be part of the group. Ambiguous names for Teams mean that members can be unsure if they need to participate or not. Clear, direct Team names aligned specifically to the purpose that the Team serves reduce misunderstanding. It also helps your IT team to know why your Team exists in the first place, helping them to better manage the Microsoft Teams environment in the background.

Giving your Team a name that aligns with your purpose sets you and your peers up for success. Having your Team name aligned to your organisational structure, the department you're a member of or the location in which you're based may make the management of Teams easier for your IT team, but it doesn't necessarily serve the best interests of those who need to work together in the space.

When naming your Team, it must be readable by humans. Having lots of prefixes in front of a Team name to make life easier for IT will hamper your team's efforts to find the right Team to participate in at the right time. Consider how people will read your Team name. If you are in a country where you read left to right, the most important or distinguishing features of the name should be as early as possible on the left-hand side. A good example we worked through recently was with a university. Should the course or unit code be first, or should the name of the subject be first?

Why is this important? Most people using Microsoft Teams will only see the first 15–20 characters of a Team name when they have Microsoft Teams open on their desktop, and even fewer characters if it is open on their mobile phone. The name that you pick for your Team should help to distinguish quickly between the different Teams you are a member of. Being a member of 13 Teams that all start with "[CORP][MKT][HQ]—Team name," "Marketing Team—Inbound," or "Marketing Team—Content" will not help you achieve that.

While we recommend that you don't front-load your Team name with too much unnecessary information, there is one important signal that should be included in a Team name, and that's whether someone from outside your organisation is participating in the Team. We will cover the reason for this in the next chapter, focused on the third P—People.

Key Takeaways

1. Don't just recreate your organisational structure; think about purposeful collaboration
2. Have one, clear purpose, per Team
3. Make sure your Team name represents your shared purpose (in fewer than 50 characters).

End of Chapter Checklist

o Refine your purpose and fill in Step 2 of the 10Ps workbook
o Then, add the name for your Team into the name box.

PEOPLE

Great things in business are never done by one person. They're done by a team of people.

—*Steve Jobs*

"Teamwork makes the dream work." "There is no I in team." "TEAM stands for Together Everyone Achieves More." There are dozens more corny lines that managers have used over time to inspire their people to come together and achieve more. Having the best one-liner will not set you up for success but having the right people on your team will. That is true for your real-life team just as much as it is for the Team that you are setting up in Microsoft Teams.

While we have all been members of our fair share of bad teams over the years—the nightmares of some group projects in high school still haunt me today—the experience of being a member of a well-oiled, highly-functioning team is incredible. In our experience, the best teams are those made up of people who come from a variety of perspectives, backgrounds, cultures and values, with a clear purpose and commitment to giving everyone a voice in the conversation. Establishing a successful team takes deliberate effort, and most managers don't get the opportunity to form or re-form teams all that regularly, maybe once every three years when there's a restructure, or when you get the chance to establish a new business unit. Or, when you get that big promotion to department head. While embracing technology like Microsoft Teams will not *ensure* your success, it will give you the opportunity to practice your craft in forming successful teams far more often and provide you with the tools to make teamwork more seamless. Every time you seek to solve a business problem or bring people together for a shared purpose, you will have the opportunity to establish effective teamwork with a new group of people and technology that can help amplify their impact.

In an organisation, there are different rules of thumb as to how many people should be in a team. You may think that throwing more people at a problem would make life easier. Some suggest that larger teams reduce the likelihood of micromanagement. Robin Dunbar, a British anthropologist, researched primate brain size and average social group size. Using the average size of a human brain as a yardstick, he suggested that a human can maintain 150 stable relationships with others.

On the other hand, some people simply like to work in small groups, or even on their own. Researchers from Wharton, Harvard and other respected institutions suggest that the sweet spot (depending on the focus of the team) is between four and nine members. My favourite is the "two pizza rule" that Jeff Bezos implemented at Amazon. If a team cannot be fed with two pizzas, then it is too big.

One important concept to consider from the field of applied psychology is the Ringelmann effect. Named after French agricultural engineer, Maximilien Ringelmann, the

Ringelmann effect describes how individual motivation decreases as team size increases. The classic example provided is a tug-of-war. Conventional wisdom would say that the more people that pull on the end of the rope, the more effort is applied. Interestingly, as the effect describes, as more people join your team to pull on the rope, the average effort of each participant significantly decreases. As individual output is less identifiable, people tend to rely more on their team members to get the job done versus putting in the effort themselves. The more people in your team, the more inefficient the team (Ringelmann, 1913).

Which begs the question: why can you create a team in Microsoft Teams that has up to *FIVE THOUSAND* members in it? Should we be creating Teams where we can have dozens, hundreds, or even thousands of participants, just because we have technology that can help us connect that number of people together? Or should we take a more practical approach?

In this chapter, we will explore some considerations of who should be a member of a Team, how many members you should have, and what roles and responsibilities lie within the Team.

At first glance, it might seem obvious who should be part of your Team but questioning how you could set up your Team gives rise to alternative approaches, all of which have merit. If you need convincing that different approaches exist, count how many of the patterns outlined later in this book have some relevance to your team.

Getting the Right People on Your Team

A team requires team members. There's no two ways about it. But, let's face it, you're realising that people are overwhelmed at work and possibly frustrated with technology. Telling them, "hey, I'll add you as a team member to my Team," without setting up some context for them is likely to result in little to no support or engagement from them.

To be successful, you need to spend some time thinking about the right people for your Team. That is, they must be empowered and engaged and have a common ground in solving a work problem, to help you achieve your shared purpose. They may come from the same department or across business units, they may be inside or outside your company, or they could be in similar or different roles. Regardless, the people you select will make or break your project, so it's worth investing time in this consideration.

Where Do You Start?

First things first: don't fall into the trap of "voluntelling" people to become involved in your Team because of the misconception that it will save you time if you force people to get involved. All you're doing is disrespecting their time and expertise. You're going to struggle to find common ground right from the beginning of the Team's formation, because they had no choice in getting involved.

Similarly, you don't always have to make the choice about who needs to be part of your Team. You may be pleasantly surprised to hear who others believe may have more of a vested interest in the Team outcomes. Conducting a short, half-hour meeting to decide to who needs to be part of the Team will provide you with a starting point for determining the right people for your Team and will also give you the confidence and authority you need to introduce your project and seek their support and contribution.

This will make your job easier, because you're asking for them to support and contribute to something that will mean a gain for them. That is, their participation will also help solve a problem for them.

What If You Can't Find the Right People?

In our experience, when you can't find the right people for your Team, there's usually something else at play. It's not that you can't find the right people, but it may be that you have not adequately diagnosed the problem and therefore may not have defined a clear purpose.

Use the earlier chapters in the book to outline the problem you need to solve, reflect on the people who may be most affected or impacted by this problem, and then ask them about it.

For example, imagine you had to build a Team to solve a problem. The problem centres on merging the details of additional staff members into your Human Resources Information System, because your company recently merged with another company. In this case, you may need to consider Team members who come from your HR team and IT team, but also the other company's HR and IT teams. You may need to also consider inviting the HR technology vendor to be involved, especially if the team identifies a need to customise system requirements. You may need to invite staff members of both companies to provide feedback on the user experience of the system. You may also need to invite the senior HR and technology managers of both companies to participate, as they are stakeholders, too.

So, can you see how widely you must consider the matter of who should be on your Team? Ultimately, they must be people who have common ground and a vested interest in the project.

When selecting the members of your Team, don't just default to your organisation's structure or the people immediately around you. Your organisation is a microcosm of diverse perspectives and experiences that generally remains untapped. Others working in different teams, business units or organisations outside of your company should not be forgotten.

You Have the Right People in the Room: What's Next?

Congratulations. You've made it this far. You have a group of people with genuine interest in and motivation to be part of your Team, and they're ready to contribute their ideas, begin conversations, collaborate on solutions, and create something that will help support the business in some way.

The next thing we need to consider is "should we break up this Team?"

"Umm. What, now? You want me to break up this Team of 43 people we have handpicked from across our organisation and our external partners?"

Yes. Yes, we do. Even though it is tempting to create a Team for your project or initiative and throw everyone into the one group, there is some complexity and nuance that you need to consider if you want to set yourself up for success with Microsoft Teams. Ultimately, it boils down to one thing: information security.

As a member of a Team in Microsoft Teams, you have the same level of access to conversations and files as everyone else in your Team. This is a great start, and far better than the siloed nature of individual mailboxes across your organisation. However, the information or security needs of Team members can vary.

For example, imagine you manage a team of 20 people, and have three team leaders as direct reports. The conversations you want to have with your team leaders will be different from those you may share with the entire group. How do you configure your Team so you can have a more private conversation with your leadership team?

When Microsoft Teams was first released, the two options you had were to 1) set up a simple group chat between yourself and your team leaders, or 2) create a separate Team just for your team leaders. The former is okay for simple communication but lacks the ability to create channels to focus the conversation. The latter means being a member of two Teams. Today, based on popular demand via Microsoft's UserVoice account (where you can suggest or support improvements to Microsoft products, including Microsoft Teams), Microsoft has added the ability to create a "private channel."

Private channels are perfect for the scenario we have painted above. You have a Team of people, but there is one subset of the group where you want to have a more secure conversation that can't be seen by the others. Another example may be where you create a Team that includes external participants, and you want to have a channel where you and your colleagues can discuss topics without those external guests seeing the conversation taking place.

While private channels make a lot of sense in these examples, it may be better to create a separate Team or Teams instead, as the information or communications needs change across your group. The beauty of a clearly named Team is that you quickly build a mental model in your mind of who is a member of that Team, and therefore what they can see. By adding one private channel, you can maintain that mental model (for example, the team I manage can see most things, but my team leaders can see all things). If you add a second, third, or fourth private channel to address the needs of *different* subgroups, then that mental model gets complex very quickly. The result? You or one of your colleagues may end up sharing the wrong information into the wrong channel, and accidentally disclosing something you didn't intend to.

At the time of publishing this book, private channels also lack the ability to schedule meetings, or add a private Planner plan, which may impact their value for your specific use cases.

Our rule of thumb is that if you have one larger group of people and one subgroup that has different security or access needs, use a private channel. If you have two or more subgroups, it is best to split them up into separate Teams.

Based on the people you need to include in your initiative and their different information needs, you may now have one, two, or more Teams. Don't be afraid of having more Teams. As you will discover over time, this will give you more fine-grained control over how you engage in these collaboration and coordination spaces. You can control notifications more easily, and identify when someone needs your help more quickly. Microsoft Teams basically starts automatically filtering work into nice, discrete buckets, without you needing to do the filtering yourself.

Assigning Roles and Responsibilities

There are different roles in a Team. Assigning roles and responsibilities is relatively easy in Teams because there are effectively only two roles that can be assigned to people: owner or member.

Someone designated as a member cannot edit any Team details, add new members, or delete a Team; however, they can do everything else, such as add channels, tabs, connectors, and even bots. Someone who is designated as an owner can do all of the above and more, like adding or removing participants from the group. You can apply some fine-grained control over what your Team members and Team owners can do through the settings for your Team.

Of course, there are slight changes to the activities that these roles can do, depending on whether your Team is public or private; however, in effect, being a Team member doesn't hinder someone's participation in and ability to work within a Team. If a member needs additional responsibilities, they can always ask the Team Owners or the IT administrator to upgrade their role

Therefore, one consideration you will need to make is to decide who in your Team needs to be a Team owner and who needs to be a member.

We recommend that you approach this from a task point of view. Ask yourself:

- What are the likely tasks this person will need to undertake in the Team?
- What level of access do they need to information or resources such as files, folders, and documents?
- Are they going to play an active role in the decision-making or leadership of the Team that will require them to have access to more functionality within the Team, or to administer functions on behalf of others in their Team?
- Are they aware of their roles and responsibilities towards the Team and/or its administration?
- Will they require some levels of control or moderation of information sharing?

By considering the role that everyone plays in the Team through a task view, you're better able to assign the appropriate role to each member.

One thing we encourage you to do is to make sure that you have a few owners for your team as a backup. That way, if the owner leaves the organisation or your Team, there are others who can take their place to ensure that all functions can still be undertaken (don't worry, IT can always step in if all the owners leave a Team).

Of course, don't spring this role on unsuspecting Team members. It's a good idea to get their commitment to be Team owners before you assign them to the role and explain what additional functionality they have access to. They need to know this because they may be asked by others to undertake some additional activities, such as answer requests to add more members to the Team or be involved in how the Team is set up or archived once completed. They may also need some coaching or a demonstration of how they can do this for themselves.

What About Moderating Conversations?

We often get asked about what happens when conversations go awry in the Team channels and how you can moderate these.

In practice, it doesn't happen all that often; however, there are some specific use cases where you may not want anyone to reply to a post, or when you just want to make announcements to a Team without the noise of responses. There's no best practice on setting up how conversations will happen. There's only *your* team's way. In the chapter on Principles, we will also guide you on what you can do to guide how your team members engage within your Team.

But, this issue is not just about conversations. It's also about how the Team has been set up.

Every team is different, and, depending on the various decisions around the 10Ps, you're going to find that there's a multitude of ways to use Microsoft Teams for the purpose you want to achieve.

For example, we worked with one airline that identified that their flight and cabin staff were so overwhelmed with email communication that they were unable to keep up with company and flight announcements.

As a result, the company decided to create a Microsoft Team and broadcast only the priority communications through a few channels. This way, the expectation of flight staff was that if they didn't have time to read email, their main way of acquiring knowledge was through Teams. They didn't interact with or engage in the channels, as they were simply a means to stay on top of important information.

This reduced the various channels of communication in the company—intranet, email, and social networks—to a handful of Teams channels that grouped key alerts together.

This example demonstrates an alternative way of using Microsoft Teams by using channel moderation. Moderation provides a level of control over what is being shared and is usually provided to certain Team members.

Team owners have this function by default; however, members have it turned off. Channel moderators can start new posts, add and remove members, and control whether members, bots, and connectors can submit and reply to messages.

Moderation does have a place in teamwork because we must consider the overall purpose and intent of the Team itself.

In the example above, the intention was to provide up-to-date company information that wouldn't overwhelm flight and cabin staff at a time when they needed it the most. It saved them time, as they no longer had to search across multiple platforms, and didn't add any additional anxiety or stress before their flights. So, with this example in mind, consider what kind of information your people need and structure your Team to suit.

In this chapter, we explored some ways to search for the right people to be involved in your Team, and looked at assigning their key roles and responsibilities.

Let's face it, teamwork is not about the technology; it's about people helping people to achieve a common goal. Making sure that you spend the time choosing the right people to solve pesky business problems will ensure your Team's implementation is a success.

Key Takeaways

1. Consider who you want to be part of your Team Ensure that all Team members have a common ground and interest to solving the problem at hand
2. In most cases, the smaller the Team, the better. Don't be afraid to break a large Team into a smaller one,

as not all the conversations or topics in a large Team will be relevant to all members

3. Consider the roles and responsibilities of your Team members. Clarify the tasks they would need to undertake and assign these accordingly. Don't forget to seek their approval prior to the assignment and coach them in or demonstrate any tasks they would need to undertake as part of their role

4. Consider whether your Team members need an additional level of responsibility for the control of information within the channels to provide moderator functions.

End of Chapter Checklist

- ○ Think about the information needs of your team. If there is more than one subgroup with different needs, split into more specific Teams
- ○ Fill in Step 3 of your 10Ps workbook
- ○ If you are planning to have external guests in your team, go back to Step 2 and add "[EXT]" to the start of your Team name (just to be sure everyone knows you have guests).

PRIORITIES

A question we regularly ask in workshops is "how many priorities can you focus on at any one time?" It's an interesting exercise , as hearing the answers can offer a good overview of how aligned a team is. "Uhh…I guess ten or twelve?" is usually followed very quickly by someone else in the team that says excitedly, "No…we can only focus on one thing at a time!" The conversation generally devolves from there for the next few minutes as the group tries to determine their shared priorities.

No matter the size or shape of your team, a group collaborating and coordinating together to achieve a shared goal will likely have several priorities.

One thing we know for sure is that no one is effective when they are overwhelmed by their priorities. If you have 20, 50, 100 or more priorities, then the chances are that you will dilute your attention so much that you will not get everything done.

In fact, research conducted by PricewaterhouseCoopers (PwC) and published by Harvard Business Review in 2011 suggested that there is a correlation between the number of priorities an organisation has and their reported revenue growth. The fewer priorities an organisation had, the greater the percentage of respondents that reported above-industry average revenue growth. Those organisations that had not prioritised at all were the worst growth performers (Mainardi & Mainardi, 2011).

When it comes to the priorities of your Team, we believe that the sweet spot is somewhere between three and seven things. If you have fewer than three priorities, you may not be structuring your work in the most effective way to allocate your resources or discretionary efforts required to achieve your goal. If you have any more than seven priorities, you are likely to overwhelm yourself and your Team with all the things that need to be focused on.

This is important to consider when establishing your Team in Microsoft Teams. As described in Part One, when you set up your Team, you can create a channel. You might like to think of a channel as equivalent to a folder that you create in Outlook or File Explorer. Instead of being a place where you can keep emails about a similar topic, or files relating to a specific area, a channel is a way to group together both your conversations and files (and other things, like tabs, that bring in third-party applications) in the one spot.

At the time of writing, you can create up to 250 channels in your Team. And we have seen many people try to hit that limit (unintentionally) by creating a channel for every possible permutation of what their team does or thinks about. When we probe the owners of these Teams to understand more about how they work in the space, we see responses from both ends of the spectrum. Either only a few of the channels see any regular engagement and the rest languish with messages that have no replies, or, worse still, there is no activity at all. Or, most of the channels are actively engaged in, but not all channels relate to all members of the Team. This leads to distraction, unnecessary notifications, and overwhelm.

So how can you set your Team up for success? First, think of three to seven priorities that you and your peers using the Team need to focus on. If you think of more than seven, we suggest it is probably worthwhile breaking your priorities into two different Teams and doing the exercise again.

Those priorities should align nicely with the channels that you set up in your Team. Think of one or two words that sum up your priority. Those words can become the name of the channel in which you focus your effort towards that priority. Make sure the channel name is clear, so everyone who joins the Team understands exactly what that channel is for and knows where to group together your conversations, files and meetings about specific topics.

Adding Some Structure or Flair to Your Channels

One of the first things you will notice as you start to add channels to your Team is that they appear in alphabetical order. While that may work in some scenarios, in others, where some are more of a priority than others, you will want to have control over the order in which the channels appear.

The General channel will always be first. Before you say, "I wish I could delete or rename the General channel," we think it is great that it stays there. As you will read about in the next chapter—Principles—the General channel has a role to play by creating a space where you can talk about *how* you work together in your Team.

After the General channel, how do we order our higher priorities a bit higher in the order of channels? As Microsoft Teams uses alphanumeric order, you can use that to your advantage. Use a simple numbering system as a prefix to your channels. Place a "1" in front of your top priority, a "2" in front of your second priority, and so on. This approach is very handy if your channels map to a customer or stakeholder journey. For the channel that maps to the first step of the journey, start the channel name with a "1"; the second step, start with a "2." You don't need to number every channel, just the ones you want to appear in order at the top of your list.

Another way you can focus on or bring attention to your channel is by adding an emoji to it. You may not be aware, but there is a virtual emoji keyboard built into Windows 10. You can open it right now, simply by holding down the Windows key and pressing the full stop button. Give it a try! You now have access to a library of different emojis or emoticons you can add to your next Word document, a presentation, or the name of a channel in Microsoft Teams. Here are a few examples: 😊 💚 👌 ✋ 🐡 🐢 🐌 🦎! We are not suggesting that you use emojis all the time. When it makes sense, and there is an emoji that relates to the focus of the channel, it is a great way to bring attention to it.

You might notice some of the screen shots we have included in the book of the Team we set up to write this book. There are four channels which are higher priority for us, in which we have included an emoji at the start of the channel name.

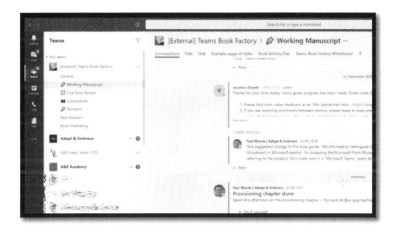

The other neat feature of using an emoji at the start of a channel name is that emojis are higher in the alphanumeric order that Microsoft Teams uses...so they will appear at the top of your channel list (just below the General channel).

What About Private Channels?

Private channels give you the ability to lock down or restrict access to conversations and files for a subset of the people in your Team. It was the most requested feature to be added to Microsoft Teams via UserVoice and was rolled out worldwide in late 2019.

As we described in the previous chapter, a simple rule of thumb for most use cases is that if you think you need more than one private channel in a Team, you are better off creating a separate team for that group of individuals to collaborate and coordinate in.

The reason we say this (apart from providing a little bit of control on what could be a land rush of private channels as people discover the feature) has to do with the data security of your work.

If you are structuring your Teams well (following the 10Ps), it will be very clear from the name of the Team what the purpose of the space is, and likely the membership of the space as well. Participants in the Team will have a mental model through which they can quickly understand who has access to what information. The members will be confident that the messages, documents, spreadsheets, presentations, meetings, and other items shared will be seen by a known group of people. As you start to introduce private channels, that mental model will start to deteriorate.

With one private channel, if you are a member of that channel, you will be able to maintain that mental model in your head. "I know that there are 14 people who are a member of this Team, and there are only four of us in the private channel." As more private channels are introduced, this will start to get complicated quickly, especially if the membership of each private channel is different. The risk of overwhelm caused by private channels is that you or your peers post conversations or files into channels where you are not 100 percent sure of the membership and potentially unintentionally expose information. They lose the confidence of knowing who has access to what, reducing trust in the system that you have put together.

Key Takeaways

1. Avoid just adding channels to your Team. Stop and think about the priorities for your group
2. Aim for 3-7 priorities (and therefore channels) for your Team
3. If you have any more than seven priorities, think about splitting the Team into two or more Teams (as chances are not everything on your list is a priority for everyone)
4. Use numbers or emojis as prefixes to structure the order in which your channels appear
5. Don't overuse or abuse private channels. Chances are, if you have more than one private channel, you would be better off setting up a separate Team for that group of people.

End of Chapter Checklist

o Not everything is a priority for everyone. If you have more than seven priorities on your list, consider splitting into two or more Teams. This will enable your people to better filter their attention throughout their work days
o Make sure that the channel names you use to represent those priorities are short and clear
o Use numbers or emojis to ensure that channels appear at the top of the channels list
o Fill in Step 3 of your 10Ps workbook.

PRINCIPLES

enry Ford once said, "Coming together is a beginning. Keeping together is progress. Working together is success."

In this book, we provide a framework for how you can be successful in working together. After all, we don't doubt that you have worked in successful teams in your work or with your interests outside of work. But, have you worked in a team that had to plan; coordinate; manage internal and external customers, stakeholders and team members across different time zones and geographical locations; *and*, use a multitude of different software programs, tools, and technology that happen to be enterprise systems?

The answer is likely to be no, which is why you're probably relying on email as your main communication method in this context. Successful teams require something more than just the tools. Sure, tools help with communication, but good teams also need a set of principles to underpin not only *how* they work but *why* they work in this way.

Jurgen Appelo, who writes about agile teams, defined principles as different to team values, saying that "With team principles, you describe the concrete focus and guideposts for your team. Principles are not the same thing as values. With team values, you describe the non-negotiable, axiomatic truths for your team." (Appelo, 2017)

In this chapter, we will provide you with those guideposts that you need to consider with your Team. These will provide your team with a way to ensure that they consistently align to what you want to achieve. Having these principles discussed, defined, and written down will ensure that everyone knows the rules of engagement and all parties have an equal voice in determining how they will work together, how information is shared, how conflict and problems are resolved and how they will capture key lessons.

Team principles will ensure that your team operates from a place of mutual trust and respect, which will drive participation and, ultimately, performance.

Where Do You Start?

The best starting place to determine your principles is to ask the team the following questions and have a deep discussion around how they would like to operate. The questions are:

- How will we communicate?
- How will we collaborate?
- How will we resolve issues and concerns?

Within each of the questions, you will need to consider the details of how participants will write a post in the Teams channel every day. However, this may not be adequate, as it doesn't consider the context of the work.

Effective communication is specific. That is, what will you write? When will you write it? Is an emoji considered a response? Do you want a reaction or a long form response? Also, the above statement does not take into account the multitude of ways that communication can happen in Teams beyond text.

For example, responses can be in different forms such as video, graphics, links to other Microsoft applications and programs like SharePoint, GIFs and many more.

Accordingly, it's evident that determining the principles of how your team communicates, collaborates and resolves conflict is critical. It will not only mean a change in the habits and behaviour of your team members, but may also require them to break out of their comfort zone, where their work will be open to their colleagues for comment, feedback and discussion.

Similarly, their work is now presented in forms other than text, such as video. This means they will have a variety of forms of expression that are different to those they've had in the past. The medium has changed from written to visual communication. This is something that some of your team members may struggle with initially, especially if they're not used to this way of communicating and collaborating. Therefore, having a set of principles by which you operate and engage with each other in the Team is important, as it takes a new commitment to how work is done, and it requires everyone's involvement.

How Will We Communicate and Collaborate?

The first question to ask and determine as a team is how you will communicate and collaborate.

You will need to decide that Microsoft Teams will now be the only platform used to share information, make decisions, and capture team project files, documents, and presentations. It will be difficult to work as a cohesive team if some members insist on continuing to use email. Therefore, take note of those who prefer to stay with email and explore their reasons for its continued use. In our experience, reluctance to embrace new technology, such as Microsoft Teams, is because they may need additional support, guidance, or coaching to use the new system or technology. Let's not forget that email has been around since the 1970s and in popular usage in the workplace since the 1990s. It's what many people have used for their entire work lives.

Resistant people may be receptive to the idea of open communication and collaboration or reducing their email inbox, but fearful of changing a habit. It's also possible that changing the systems they've set up to manage their inbox may override their need to participate in and contribute to Microsoft Teams.

Recently we worked with a client who we will call Jan. Jan was an administrative assistant and a long-time employee of a financial services company. Over the years of working in the company, Jan had developed an extensive set of manual and paper-based processes around travel authorisations and staff requests for travel, all conducted through email. She was placed in a Microsoft Team as a team member and, at the outset, seemed excited to be involved—if not daunted by the online environment—and interested in learning a new program that would help her manage and coordinate her work.

However, when she realised that the processes that she'd been doing through these years had to change and she was now required to complete these tasks within Teams, her demeanour changed. Suddenly, she became anxious that she would lose track of her requests, that she wouldn't be able to know the progress of her work and that she couldn't trust that people would follow her procedure. Jan also questioned the openness and transparency of Microsoft Teams, fearing that it was akin to losing privacy and control of her work.

As a result, she sought permission from her manager to continue using her manual systems through email. Her team acknowledged that she was feeling lost, not only about the process change but also about how this change would impact the work she'd been doing for many years. Her team rallied around her and provided her with additional coaching and desk support. They showed her how she could use Microsoft Teams to streamline her work, step by step. The additional coaching provided Jan with the opportunity to build trust with Microsoft Teams (and her team members) and contribute to her Team effectively.

In time, Jan realised that the introduction of Microsoft Teams was not due to her company's management or her team taking personal aim at her work. Instead, it was to alleviate tedious tasks so that she could focus on providing more value through her ideas and insights into the team.

At first, Microsoft Teams can be seen as an addition to every other work system you have, not as a replacement. In the example above, Jan misunderstood the intent of Microsoft Teams as being the platform that replaces email, not another system to use for that one project she was assigned. This is where you and your team will need to ensure that all members are aware of these distinct differences and are supported in their use and application.

Let's look at some ways you can decide how you will communicate.

Types of Posts and Conversations

You can discuss the types of conversations and posts you will all contribute to and create a principle around these. For example, you may decide that your team will avoid posting in the General channel and reserve this only for communications about how you work together as a Team. Instead, new channels of conversations can be created around specific themes. In this way, conversations are focused in the correct channel rather than sprawled across the General channel.

Ask your team:

- What are the types of conversations and posts we can write and share?
- How will the General channel be used?

- What are the main topics of conversations or themes that this team will use so that we can align channels with these?
- How will we edit and annotate the posts so they don't get lost in the threads?
- How can we ensure the right people are added or mentioned in conversations they need to be a part of?
- How can we ensure conversations continue as threads: replying to posts as opposed to starting new conversations?
- How can we ensure that our replies, posts, and comments always add value, that is, they're educational, insightful, thoughtful, and relevant to the discussion?

When writing this book, the *Adopt & Embrace* team used various channels for the conversations around how we were planning, writing, and editing the manuscript, as shown in the screenshot. The channels were based around the themes of the book.

We used the General channel for team announcements. The Working Manuscript channel housed all our conversations about our individual work for each chapter, while the Coaching Review channel held conversations with our book coach regarding the editing, proofing, and review of our drafts.

You can see that we also captured information regarding screen shots and research in one place so that we could easily find them. Finally, the Beta Reader and Book

Marketing channels contained conversations with external members of our organisation who could also contribute their feedback.

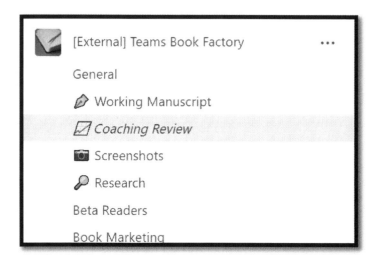

Use of 1:1 Chat for Back-Channel Conversations

In your team, discuss how you see one-to-one conversations happening. For example, you may decide that any conversation regarding a task between two individuals pertaining to the project is made open and placed in the appropriate channel, rather than using the more private 1:1 chat. This way, the work can be found by others who need it.

This is particularly useful when one team member is absent or to bring a new staff member up to speed.

Therefore, direct messaging to others is reserved only for private and confidential matters.

Ask your team:

- How will we use chat?
- When is a chat message deemed information that should be shared to the Teams channel for everyone's information?

Use of Mentions and Notifications

Microsoft Teams allows you to set up your Teams and channels any way you like. However, there is also an area in Settings where you can individualise your team's experience. Your team may need guidance to set this up because we all work differently.

We all want to create the experience of how we enter and use Teams so that it integrates with our own way of working and flows. For example, some Team members may not like to have notifications emailed to them, so they have the flexibility to personalise the experience by turning these off. Similarly, some people like to have some notifications turned off so they're only notified for certain critical conversations they're following.

During your team discussion to set up principles, discuss how you can set up notifications, too. Initially, you may decide to have notifications turned on so that it triggers an action, like a behaviour for your team member to remember to use Microsoft Teams for their work. Over time, as your team members become comfortable using the settings, they may alter them to suit their new workflow. Similarly, you will need to educate your Team about the use of the @ symbol—or the mention.

This symbol is used when you want to mention someone. Think of it as a prompt—like calling someone's name across a crowded room—where you direct someone's attention to the conversation. Mentioning a person, the whole channel or the whole Team in Microsoft Teams can be powerful if used well, as it will (by default) notify the person or people you mention that they need to look at a message. If it is overused, however, the power of a mention disappears quickly. If I am getting notified 37 times a day just because someone is replying to me, I am more likely to ignore a mention, as opposed to when I'm mentioned twice in a day and only when someone is asking me to take an action.

Our rule of thumb (as mentioned in Part One) is that you only mention someone in a post *if* you want them to do something explicitly based on that message. Don't just mention them if you want them to read it as an FYI, because if you do that, everyone will be overwhelmed with notifications in no time.

Ask your team:

- Does everyone know how to use mentions?
- What are the rules of use for mentions in conversations and Teams?
- How can people set up their notifications?
  - Do you want to encourage people to set them up for the purpose of the Team or in their own preferred way?
- Where will critical and important announcements be made so that people can see these, despite having notifications turned off?

When to Start New Conversations and When to Continue Conversations

Microsoft Teams enables you to provide a rich experience of communication and collaboration, compared to email. In an email, you can attach a file, provide some context about that file and send it through to your recipient. Once they receive it, they can add another file, provide additional context, and send it on. However, in little time, this process results in a long email thread which is as unwieldy as it is unsearchable, creating frustration.

By comparison, in Microsoft Teams, you upload a file in a channel and have all the conversations centred around that file in its own conversation space. It reduces the dreaded email trees and allows everyone to have the same view of the file and the conversations around it.

Another benefit is that Microsoft Teams allows for separate conversations to happen within channels, which email cannot do. This way, important information is easily accessible and isn't lost in long threads, which improves staff productivity.

Having conversations around documents in Microsoft Teams is something new to many people, and we encourage you to discuss how new conversations are added to the channel. Rather than start a new conversation, your team needs to learn a new behaviour of searching to see if that conversation has already happened so they can continue the thread of conversation rather than start a new conversation, if applicable.

To do this, type the conversation topic in the search bar. If you don't find what you're looking for, you can start a new conversation.

In the screenshot below, I'm searching for anything with the word "chapters" in it. Teams shows me all the messages where the word "chapters" is located. I can filter these further if I need to. Once I find what I'm looking for, then I'm able to go directly to that conversation. If I cannot find the specific conversation I'm looking for, or if the search does not yield any results, I can now start a new thread.

This process is a great way to ensure that conversations are grouped and themed and do not lead to separate and disparate threads that are not connected or linked. It also keeps the channel tidy.

Ask your team:

- Is your team familiar with the search function?
- What are the rules around starting new conversations versus replying to conversations?
- Is the team aware of how to create links to tabs, documents, and files?

Providing Context for Conversations

Once your team starts using Microsoft Teams, the conversations will build over time and may start to look disordered. For some, this is going to take a while to get used to, but in our experience, we have noticed that people soon start to follow what others are doing, especially if the information is presented in a way that helps them to quickly find what they're looking for. One of the ways to do this is to encourage your Team members to provide context for their conversations.

Context refers to the provision of additional or supporting information that enables someone else to achieve an outcome more quickly. This could mean providing a direct link to a specific document in the conversation, @mentioning the people who need to take action in the conversation, or linking the conversation to a previous conversation in Teams. This minimises the time people need to search for information or context.

That way, you're cross-referencing and linking together disparate pieces of information in Microsoft Teams into the one conversation. It is not only a time saver but also shows respect for the person reading it, because you're providing them with all the information they need without them having to back-track and glean the information from multiple conversation threads.

Therefore, consider making one of your principles that, when your Team members contribute to the conversation, they provide cross-referencing or links to supporting documents, files, and conversations for more context.

Ask your team:

- Do we know how to create links to files, documents, and tabs in Microsoft Teams?
- How will we cross-reference and link to files, documents, and tabs to create context around conversations in Microsoft Teams?

Providing Status Updates

A key function of any Team is to provide status updates, and these can occur in several ways. There is no right or wrong way to do this, nor is there a best practice, as these are indicative of how your team prefers to do this.

At *Adopt & Embrace*, we have both external Microsoft Teams, where we directly collaborate with our customers (for example, the planning, coordination, and writing of this book was conducted entirely in Teams), as well as internal Teams, where, together with our peers, we discuss and plan customer work.

As we work on projects where our colleagues rely on information, we have decided that every time we undertake work at a client site, we provide a status update in the relevant channel.

This way, other Team members can see what work we have completed, what issues we highlighted, and what work remains to be done. It allows people to get a quick snapshot of what transpired. Details of the project are captured in the relevant channel with appropriate links to further information.

Consider how your team can provide status updates and what these may look like. Other Teams we have seen have created a specific channel for Status Updates where every member can contribute their reports. Others prefer a more formalised structure to their status updates for team meetings, with agenda and briefing points in, for example, OneNote notebooks that are then linked to in conversations in Teams.

Ultimately, the different ways to provide status reports are unending; however, as a principle of coordinating your teamwork, you need to discuss and decide on this as a team.

With Microsoft Teams, you now have a variety of ways to do this, so why not be creative? Here's your opportunity to make status reports something more memorable, something that people *want* to provide.

Ask your team:

- How will we provide status updates to other Team members and those people outside of our Team who may need to know the status of our project?

Sending Emails to Channels

Earlier, we mentioned that using Microsoft Teams will involve new behaviour for some of your team. The biggest hurdle you will face is weaning Team members off email and moving their work to Teams.

There are many articles and posts online claiming the demise and death of email; however, to date, this has not been the case. Although we cannot foresee the future, what we have seen with the companies with which we work is that, upon the introduction of Microsoft Teams into the workplace, the volume of emails reduces; however, email doesn't disappear entirely.

That is, there will be times when people default to sending email about their team project. They may still have external parties or stakeholders who are not Team members or privy to the conversations in the channel. Email, in this case, is still a viable form of communication, especially if it's used one-to-one. In these situations, it's important that, as a team, you clarify how people will use email and encourage the sharing of that email back into the Team channels of conversation.

Therefore, a principle you may decide on as a team is one for "transparent work" that involves sending all emails related to team projects into the Team. Demonstrate that every Team's channel has its specific email address and encourage people to add this email address as a CC: when they're sending out emails to customers and stakeholders. A copy of this email will then be sent to the appropriate Team's channel so that everyone on the team can see what has been sent.

Ask your team:

- How will we ensure that all emails related to the project are redirected back into the relevant Team channel for everyone to view and comment on?
- Is there anyone outside of our team who needs to have access to this response in email (and access to the Team resources) to reduce the use of email to them?
- Are the above people internal or external to our organisation (as you may have different rules for Team members who are not employees)?

Video Recordings of Team Meetings

Let's face it, managing relationships, and therefore meetings, are a part of life. People who work together will need to meet in person and/or online in order to plan, coordinate, and manage their team's project.

Where meetings in Microsoft Teams differ is how they can be conducted. That is, they can be conducted synchronously (participants communicate in real time) or asynchronously (participants communicate over a period). This means that everyone can participate and contribute to the meeting experience, regardless of whether they are there in person or not. This is achieved using the recording feature, which enables the meeting to be recorded and reviewed later.

For example, a Team member who is ill on the day of a team meeting can instead watch the recording of the meeting so that he or she is across the actions discussed. Similarly, if your colleague is overseas and the time zone of your meeting does not suit their time, they can watch it at a more suitable time. The recording builds inclusivity into your team, making geographical and time limitations cease to be obstacles.

Recording meetings is not a new concept. People have been recording meetings through note taking and voice recorders for years. The only difference now is that this function is available to everyone at the click of a button. Recording meetings may not sit well with some of your Team members and this is where you may need to discuss how this will happen.

A way to consider recording is to have the meeting facilitator disclose to the participants that the meeting will be recorded. If someone has an issue with meetings being recorded, you can then explore the objection and find the reasons why. You may decide in that instance that the meeting will not be recorded. In our experience, many people overcome their initial anxiety when they know how the recordings will be used and where they will be shared.

You may decide, however, that not all team meetings need be recorded, and that is okay. By being transparent about the fact that the team meeting is being recorded and then automatically transferred into the appropriate channel in Microsoft Teams, everyone is included in the dialogue. The days of having to schedule an appropriate time when everyone is there or seeking out meeting minutes/information about what was discussed in team meetings are now gone!

Ask your team:

- How will we record our meetings?
- Does everyone approve of using and recording meetings for the Team?
- If not, how will we resolve any objections?

Following Channel Conversations

One of the most critical aspects of teamwork is ensuring that your team members have the right information at the right time in order to make decisions that will affect or impact the project. However, there's only so much you can do.

As a team leader, you are responsible for ensuring that your staff keep up with information so that they can make the most informed decisions. It will be your responsibility to provide support and guidance if any of your Team members struggle with this responsibility. Initially, until your team gets used to the new way of working, they may find it overwhelming. When they see how many Teams they have been assigned to, they may worry about how to keep up with the conversations in those Teams.

There are ways to manage this information overwhelm, such as demonstrating how Team members can show or hide channels within Teams and set their notifications accordingly.

Alternatively, you can show them that not all Teams are active. If there are Teams in which they do not play an active role, these Teams can be hidden from view. Show your Team how they can reorder their Teams by dragging and dropping them up and down their list to create some personal order in the vertical navigation bar.

Also, show Team members some tips, such as saving conversations (or bookmarking them) so that they can be easily found. Alternatively, and/or additionally, they can mark some conversations "unread" so that they become bolded and can therefore be found more easily, as shown below. Saved bookmarks are then collated in the Profile setting, under the title "Saved." If it is an important channel, it could be pinned to the top of the Team list.

Once again, there's no right or wrong way to do this, nor is there a best practice use of conventions around following and notifying. This convention can only be obtained after using Microsoft Teams for a while and then deciding on an individual's most preferred way to work.

As a start, however, it's wise to encourage Team members to follow and create notifications for channels of conversations that are relevant for them, and hide any Teams or channels that are not relevant to them.

Ask your team:

- How will we ensure we follow the right conversations and channels?
- How can we clear up the visual interface of our desktop so that we do our best work without distractions and clutter on the screen?

Team Channel Conventions

We have discussed different aspects to creating your Team's principles and how they relate to helping the individual to change their behaviour so that they can contribute to and participate in conversations within Teams channels rather than emails. That is, they may be communicating with people in their team who have a vested interest in a specific channel, but what are the behaviours when communications need to be sent to the entire team?

As mentioned previously in this book, we have all been on the receiving end of an email accidentally sent to everyone in the organisation. You may have been the person who sent such an email! The dreaded "reply-all" email creates a long email thread that inevitably clogs up everyone's inbox. People know that you must never "reply all" to emails or risk everyone's ire.

In Microsoft Teams, although this will not happen to such an extent (it is unlikely that an entire organisation will be in one Team unless you have set up an organisation-wide Team), it may still happen. However, the numbers would be reduced to only the members of that Team. Therefore, you may want to create some principles around restricting the use of mentions (@Team or @channel names) in conversations unless it is necessary. The alternative is to use the General tab, as mentioned above, for any Team-wide communications or general announcements. Reserve the mention for specific people instead.

Ask your team:

- How will we use the mention convention?
- Who needs to have access to our Teams channels?
- Are these people inside or outside our Team and our organisation?

Start and Stop Behaviours

We have now come to the point of looking at the new set of behaviours that your Team will be asked to demonstrate.

By now, asking the questions outlined above, your team will notice a need to flip their thinking and look at how their own workplace behaviours around teamwork and collaboration can be more open, inclusive, and supportive.

You need to decide what old behaviours will be stopped and what new behaviours need to start.

In our experience, it's worthwhile to prioritise some time to facilitate this and capture what everyone in your Team thinks. You may already have a starting point, including that today you:

STOP	START
• **Stop using email for the project** • **Stop sending emails with attachments** • **Stop uploading a file without linking it to a conversation**	• Start setting up your profile and notifications • Start using Microsoft Teams and channels • Start @mentioning someone who needs take an action • Start replying to or commenting on posts where people have something of value to add • Start showing channels of interest to your work and hiding those that don't

Ask your team:

- What are some of the start and stop behaviours around the use of Microsoft Teams that we can start today?

Resolving Problems, Issues, and Conflict

In every Team, you're going to have various degrees of conflict, problems and issues that need to be solved. For your Team to succeed, you will need to decide on principles for resolving problems and conflicts that may arise. One consideration is that everyone will be able to participate in the resolution of the problem if it is within the Teams channel or the conversation. This means that highlighted issues can be resolved quickly through collaborative discussion and feedback.

The value of sharing issues and problems openly in the Teams channel is that everyone has an opportunity to contribute to a solution together. Ideas for how resolution may occur can be discussed and debated without anyone feeling that they may be at fault. Airing issues early in the Teams channel can also prevents issues from escalating further.

Ask your team:

- How will we resolve any problems, issues, or conflicts?
- How can we encourage people to share these openly in our Team?
- What can we do if issues aren't resolved to a satisfactory level of every Team member?

Getting it All Down in Writing (Wiki)

Your team will have collated a lot of information in responding to the questions outlined above. At *Adopt & Embrace,* we use the Wiki tab in Microsoft Teams to capture the general Team information about how that Team will work together. A "wiki" is a simple page that you can use to structure information and allow others to update over time. Wikipedia is the most famous example of a "wiki" in action. We encourage you to build out the Team principles into the wiki associated with your General channel and have everyone contribute their ideas to it. This way, this wiki can then be used as an additional resource for those members who join the Team later and need to get up to speed.

The wiki can be used as a Team induction resource that steps new members through how to use the Team and how members collaborate. It will save you time in collating resources, links, and tabs by having these all within one collaborative page that can be continually updated as information changes, and to which you can direct people so they understand the processes and principles with which your Team works. It's a great time saver!

Summary

Team principles are the rules by which you and your members will engage within the Team. Taking the time to discuss and determine your Team principles—and then writing them down—will ensure that all members know the behaviours they will display to make sure the Team operates in as smooth manner as possible. Your Team principles can change over time, so as the Team owner, it is worthwhile revisiting the discussion with your Team every three months to ensure that everyone is on the same page. As the Team owner, it is also up to you to make sure that everyone acts in accordance with the agreed principles as well. There's no need to publicly shame people, a simple 1:1 chat message or video call reminding them about how best to use the space is all that is usually needed.

Communication and collaboration in Microsoft Teams is different to email because Teams opens doors to different forms of expression and makes work more visible and discoverable. This new way of working may make some of your Team members anxious; however, we encourage coaching, guidance, and support along the way to ensure that every member plays their part in keeping the Team together.

Key Takeaways

1. Discuss, define, and write down the principles of how your Team will contribute and participate
2. Determine your start and stop behaviours and commit to these for the life of your Team
3. Encourage your Team members to continue to support each other through the new ways of working and new behaviours such as linking, video meetings, searching, and setting up their profile for notifications. Help each other set up for success.

End of Chapter Checklist

o Agree to the principles that your Team will embrace in the 10Ps Workbook
o Document those principles in a wiki tab or another document and make it available in your Team's General channel
o Fill in Step 5 of your 10Ps workbook.

PLUGINS

D on't let the word scare you. Plugins is just a fancy way of us describing the things outside Microsoft Teams that can be used to add more context or customise your communication, collaboration or coordination experience in some way.

Microsoft Teams, quite deliberately, is meant to do a lot of things. To be suitable for a wide audience, it needs to be useful across different industries, across different Team sizes, and useful no matter what type of work you do. If you think about it, it's quite hard to design a single product that is useful to a nurse, contact centre worker, repair technician, and CEO. Yet, this global appeal is what Microsoft Teams achieves.

The key to achieving broad appeal is flexibility, and plugins is how Microsoft Teams achieves this. Rather than building in niche features that only students in a classroom, or clinicians in a hospital or engineers in a construction company might use, the underlying product is a flexible blank canvas with core features that everyone will use. After that, it's up to your Team to customise it to suit your needs.

Plugins: Tabs, Connectors, Bots, and Extensions

This chapter will focus almost entirely on simple plugins that allow you to embed other products within Microsoft Office 365 into your workspace. We will also explore how to integrate web-based solutions you might already use. This is a good starting point for two reasons.

Firstly, it means that this chapter will be relevant to you. The reality for a lot of our customers is that anything more complicated than a simple tab included in your channel requires a governance discussion with your IT team. Secondly, it allows you to have a principled discussion about plugins without getting distracted by the bells, whistles, and promises of shiny new apps. Start off with the basics and understand when it makes sense to augment your Microsoft Teams experience with other tools. Then, you're in a good place to start experimenting with more advanced features, but only once you have an appreciation for what works.

What's in It for Me

Plugins are a great example of a win–win, both for the people who use the product (you) and the product development team (Microsoft). The biggest advantage to using the different styles of plugins available in Microsoft Teams is that you aren't waiting on Microsoft to create the features you want. Within reason, you can quickly collate all the resources your team frequently uses into a single shared Microsoft Teams window. You don't have to wait for Microsoft to develop, test, and gradually release new features.

One of the critical wins, from a change management perspective, is that plugins allow your most common processes to continue as-is. Provided there is a web interface, you can simply add your existing process website as a tab, and nothing much needs to change. People can continue to use the existing system in much the same way they always have, in the context of a collaboration space powered by Microsoft Teams.

The other side of the coin is that Microsoft can concentrate on developing the core features of its product, avoiding being torn in different directions by feature requests and support tickets. It allows them to produce a product that isn't too bloated, so you don't have to worry about evaluating a long list of features you never knew existed and then deciding to enable or disable them.

So, let's take a look at some of the common plugins that you will want to use inside your Team.

Tabs

Tabs are the mainstay of our plugin philosophy. Just like a tab in your browser window, a tab in Microsoft Teams allows you to switch to a different resource quickly. Think of a tab as a great way to "bookmark" a resource that is relevant to that channel.

One word of warning: keep it simple and add just one or two tabs that make sense for that channel. Adding too many tabs causes Microsoft Teams to collapse them into a drop-down:

You can add a tab by clicking the "+" to the right of the tabs, which will bring up the available tabs. Depending on your company's settings, different tabs may be available. We expect the number of available tabs to grow over time, but practically speaking, you will only be interested in a small number of them. Those would be tabs relating to tools that you already use, and from time to time, that list would be a useful starting point for searching for new or replacement tools. This is all limited by your IT security settings, if applicable.

When to Consider Tabs

Not every channel or Team needs additional tabs. There will certainly be times when the default chat and files tabs are more than enough for people to get work done in a channel. Consider a tab when:

- The purpose of the Team is clearly encapsulated in a go-to document or information source
- You regularly refer to specific documents, spreadsheets, presentations, or videos
- The Team uses web-based tool(s) regularly and consistently.

When thinking about go-to documents, there are two main categories:

1. Curated conversations: where a discussion's outcome is important but will inevitably get lost in the channel's conversation history. While the chat in Microsoft Teams is searchable, sometimes you just want to skip to the answer without needing the background. By all means, have the discussion, but collating important information in an easy-to-consume format and a known location is a much better strategy for knowledge management. Typically, that information can be placed in a OneNote, Word or wiki tab.

2. Regularly used resources: where the information needs to be "bookmarked" for easy access. This could be, for example, a PowerPoint presentation that is critical to the channel's purpose. This is often a matter of convenience—the document is probably accessible in the Files tab anyway. In the Team that created this book, we pinned the draft Word document as a tab.

You will know what external tools your team uses and which are relevant to the Team's purpose. Each Team's purpose is unique. So, for example, it makes sense to add a payroll SaaS product as a website tab for an HR team. Although they might also regularly use the same system, other Teams probably don't need that payroll system to be a tab. They key thing to remember when using the Website tab to add an external SaaS application to your channel is that the URL or web address you are pointing the tab to needs to start with https://.

Some tools might have created their own dedicated tab, which you may find in the growing library of tabs displayed when you add a tab to your channel. Otherwise, it's perfectly acceptable to use the Website tab to streamline access to web-based systems. Even if the tool has its own plugin, you may choose to pin the application as a website anyway if the plugin doesn't have the required functionality.

When to Avoid Tabs

Part of the value of Microsoft Teams is that people get the same shared view of the Team. Native Microsoft tabs generally don't allow you to break with this philosophy; for example, you can't add a list from a SharePoint site (other than the SharePoint site associated with the Team) because some people in the Team might not have access to it. Well-designed third-party plugins should continue this approach.

It is, of course, possible to break this design philosophy, and it's quite easy to unknowingly do this by adding a Website tab. Any website that requires a login opens the possibility that some Team members don't have access or might have different permissions in that external system.

The "Go-To" Tabs

OneNote

This is perfect for semi-structured knowledge management in Teams. As a place to put "static" content, OneNote is very effective in a Team context. For example, if members of your team are involved in meetings across your organisation, by using the shared OneNote notebook within your Team, you can consolidate all the meeting notes into one shared space. In fact, a OneNote is one of the standard resources created by Office 365 when a new Team is created.

The alternative to a OneNote tab is a wiki, but in our view, OneNote has far more functionality (two or more people able to edit at once and version history being two advantages), especially as you can directly open the Team's notebook from the OneNote app on your phone, tablet or computer.

Planner

Planner is a lightweight project management tool, the sweet spot between using Excel to track tasks and building out a work breakdown structure in Project. Planner is more interactive, in the sense that you can encourage people not only to consume the task schedule but also to contribute to it as well (for example, updating the completion status for their tasks).

Planner is obviously relevant for a Team where the problem at hand is related to coordination, but it's important to remember that this is a very lightweight tool. Most notably, it doesn't include versioning or a permissions model, so anyone can update any task and there is no way to see what the previous state was.

Forms

If you have any information capture or survey needs, you can quickly add a Microsoft Form tab to your channel to enable that data collection to occur. A simple surveying tool, Microsoft Forms can be used to collect information both inside and outside your organisation. Both the form design and the responses are available via the tab, enabling quick access to the insights you are gathering. You can then export the data to an Excel spreadsheet.

We used the Forms tab multiple times with the beta readers for this book: when we asked them to confirm their participation and agree to the gives and gets of being a beta reader; when we asked them for feedback on the design concepts for the cover of this book; and when we wanted their final feedback on the book itself. All that information was available to all the co-authors of the book, just by clicking on a tab in the Beta Readers channel (and not hidden away in another survey tool).

Yammer

It could be the subject of its own book—the arrangement of a complementary Team and Yammer community is one that many teams will find appealing, but it does require a bit of explanation.

Very briefly, the Team is for the core team and is the engine room of work. The Yammer community is used for outwardly sharing news and knowledge about the work the core team is doing, with interested parties across your organisation. Conversely, feedback from the Yammer community can be imported and discussed in the more private Team. Adding the Yammer tab to a channel in your Team enables this to happen more easily.

Word, Excel, and PowerPoint

It's probably a little unfair to put the rest of these in the same bucket, but from a Microsoft Teams perspective, the tabs perform much the same function. Use these to pin documents that are frequently used in a channel. Practically speaking, this only saves a few mouse clicks (you can always get to the same document through the files tab), but the people who like organisation and structure will thank you.

Apps, Bots, Connectors, Messaging Extensions, and Tabs

This section is for people who are confident with the basics and want to dive into something more advanced. If you don't think a ready-made tab fits your needs, this section briefly touches on what's available if you're game to try creating a Teams plugin yourself. If this is not you, then please skip this section!

First, let's get the fancy and confusing words out of the way. In Microsoft Teams, an app is something that includes at least one of the following:

- Bots
- Connectors
- Messaging extensions
- Tabs.

An app can include more than one of those things, and the most common combination (if you had to include more than one) would be a bot and a tab. There will be times when people are less precise with their language and when they say an "app," they probably just mean a "bot."

Next, let's understand a little more about what those things are.

Bots

Bots are software programs that interact through a chat-based conversation. In Microsoft Teams, people can interact with bots in a channel, in a group chat, or individually.

Most of the bots we hear about today are set up for individual chats, effectively as a user-friendly search or discovery interface. For example, you could ask a bot "what is my leave balance?" or "what is the address of our office in New York?" Other examples of bots are those which encourage a "check in" or response from an individual. An example could be a workplace health and safety bot which sends out an "Are you okay?" question if a safety incident occurs on a worksite. Another example could be a teaching and learning bot which checks in with students throughout the semester to gauge their understanding of the coursework (and to suggest additional reading for the areas they may be struggling with).

Bots are emerging as useful tools in the workplace; however, they do require a "keep it simple" approach. As the complexity of your requirements increases, so does the complexity of building and maintaining your bot.

Connectors

A connector is a way of bringing external events into a channel within your Team. Through the lens of adoption, this is a bit of a conundrum. The assumption is that the work continues in the external system, despite the need to import those notifications into Microsoft Teams. Yet there is often nothing to complete the loop between the two systems: taking a response in Microsoft Teams and feeding it back into the system that reported the initial event. Which brings into question what "work" is being done in Microsoft Teams as a result of this connector, because work presumably is done in the external system. The exception is if the external event is generated without human involvement, for example, an outage notification that might require a discussion about the event in Microsoft Teams.

For this reason, we would suggest that connectors be used sparingly, and only where they add to the purpose of the Team. Even then, a connector can potentially end up confusing people about which systems they should be using to get work done.

Messaging Extensions

The easiest way to understand messaging extensions is by examining how the GIF selector works (if you are reading this well after this book was first published, GIFs were a hilarious way of communicating using short animations back in 2019). When you want to add a GIF, Microsoft Teams opens a dialog box with a search bar and suggested GIFs for insertion. After searching, you can select a GIF to insert it into the message. More generally, a messaging extension allows user interaction (for example, the dialog box) before inserting content into a message.

Theoretically, the value of a messaging extension comes from its ability to include context from an external system directly into a conversation (in GIF selector, that external system is a library of GIFs). For example, you might have a third-party Patient Management System, Student Management System, or Customer Relationship Management System, and you want to add some additional information from that system into the context of your conversation. Instead of having to switch to the other application to find out the high-level information, you can have it automatically populate in your conversation as a message or card.

Tabs

Since almost any website can be added as a tab in Microsoft Teams using the built-in website type, you may be wondering about the point of creating an app with a tab.

The short answer to this is that it provides a smoother user experience, particularly where the app includes other elements (bots and connectors). When it is integrated through a dedicated app, the external system is sent information about the user and Team context, rather than having to rely on a separate login.

In order to allow a smoother user experience, the tab needs to meet certain requirements, including running various Microsoft Teams-specific scripts. Or, in other words, if you don't have control over the system's HTML, then you won't be able to develop a tab.

The perfectly acceptable workaround, if you don't have control over the source, is adding a tab using the built-in website type.

Can Anyone Create a New Plugin for Microsoft Teams?

If you or someone in your team has some development or coding experience, you could create your own bot, connector, messaging extension or tab. Check out the Microsoft Teams Developer Centre (https://developer.microsoft.com/en-us/microsoft-teams), which includes guides, templates, and training to help you create a plugin that meets your requirements.

Ultimately, Office 365 administrators have control over which apps people can add, regardless of whether they're published publicly or developed internally. Before embarking on developing an app for your Team, it's worth checking that internally developed apps are allowed within your Tenant, or at the very least that you have a process to engage with governance decision-makers and potentially whitelist (specifically allow) your app.

Key Takeaways

1. Add tabs to Teams as bookmarks
2. Only add tabs where they are relevant to the purpose of the Team and channel
3. Even if your SaaS product has a Teams app, don't assume it will have the exact functionality you want or need
4. Don't get caught up in the hype of apps and bots— think about the other Ps first and plugins become the icing on the cake.

End of Chapter Checklist

○ In your 10Ps workbook, write down up to three things that will add context for each of your channels. It could be a document, notebook, spreadsheet, video, or third-party system
○ Add them as tabs to your Team.

PERMISSIONS

"I'm wondering if you can help me, Helen?" asked a client on the phone one day.

I had received a bit of good news about a client and decided to give him a call and speak to him rather than send a message electronically. Besides, as a remote worker, I wanted to chat with someone. I hoped that I could catch him at his desk or that he answered his phone. Amusingly, I thought, "that's the danger of the modern workplace, when people don't answer their calls or let them go to voice mail!"

To my delight, he answered, and as we laughed about the "old-fashioned approach" of having a phone discussion, the conversation was light-hearted and friendly. He used the opportunity to ask a question that was concerning him and his business team about how some external team members (who are not a part of his organisation) could not access a team plan.

"These people are from another company; however, they work closely with our internal marketing team on joint projects. They can't seem to access the Planner that assigns them the tasks and activities they need to do. They get an error message. We've looked at all the permissions of both Microsoft Teams and the Microsoft Planner, but it has us stumped. They just don't see what our people see. Any recommendations for what we could do?"

This problem made me think about how our work happens as part of a team and how, sometimes, we forget the people, teams, and companies that are outside of our organisation and with whom we need to work to achieve business outcomes.

If they sit outside our organisation and are still part of a project team—are they still considered part of our Team?

Of course they are. However, in the past, this was hindered by the considerations of technology and platform limitations between the parties as well as the security of the information.

For example, imagine an internal marketing team working with an external advertising agency. The agency may be using other suites of products within the Google or Apple ecosystem and will need to send information back and forth to their corporate client, who may be using the Microsoft suite. Meanwhile, the corporate organisation may need certain information from their advertising agency and will need them to use their own systems. This is where Microsoft Teams comes into play. Both parties can communicate and achieve their team outcomes by accessing the Team space for discussions as well as links to the relevant files for that project. It reduces the need to email information back and forth between parties and duplicate the effort to input information into different ecosystems.

This means that, for Team members to collaborate and work together on projects, they all play different roles within the team and as such, will need to have different permissions for access and use of the information that is in the Team. This is the topic of this chapter.

How to Define Permissions in Microsoft Teams

The topic of defining permissions is likely to generate some discussion when you first set up your Team, because you'll need to have a clear idea of not only the purpose of your Team and the problem that you're solving but also the people who are part of your Team. These people may sit both inside and outside your organisation, and yet, as a Team member, Microsoft Teams does not distinguish this. A Team member is a Team member regardless of whether they sit inside or outside your company.

You will need to consider what information is available and what can be made available to them, and then make an assessment as to whether you need more granular control over who can access files and other content.

Ask yourself:

- Do you want external guests accessing all company-specific files in that Team?
- Do you want sensitive and private conversations between parties available to everyone in the Team to read and comment?
- Do you want Team members to be able to edit or delete files and conversations in the Teams?

Permissions in Microsoft Teams

What are the permissions that you can set for your members in Teams? You can:

- Create and update channels
- Allow members to delete and restore channels
- Create, update, and remove tables
- Create, update, and delete connectors
- Add and remove bots
- Everyone can delete their messages
- Everyone can edit their messages

In the General Channel:

- Anyone can post messages
- Anyone can post; show alert that posting will notify everyone
- Only owners can post

Guest Permissions:

- Enable channel creation
- Allow creation and update of channels
- Allow guests to delete channels

Use of @Mentions

- Allow @team or @[team name] mentions—this will send a notification to everyone in the Team
- Allow @channel or @[channel name] mentions—this will send a notification to everyone who has favourited the channel being mentioned

Use of Giphy

- Allow use of emojis, GIFs, and stickers
- Filter out inappropriate content settings

We recommend that when you are working with your Team that you encourage them to go through each of the above permissions and to explore the following…

Does this permission:

- Allow our Team members to do what they need to do without adding additional work, frustration, or obstacles to achieve their Team outcomes?
- Provide them with the right level of access and authority in their role in the Team?
- Allow them to access information we are comfortable to share with them? (That is, is it aligned to the company IT policy around file sharing?)

Summary

Determining permissions is not an onerous task, but it does need some consideration when it comes to considering the roles of the various people in your Team and what you want them to do as well as what resources you want them to access and be able to share.

Too often, we may forget that our Teams also are made up of external agencies, contractors, vendors and suppliers who need access to the resources to allow them to undertake their side of the project. In this case, Microsoft

Teams allows different access levels to ensure that teamwork and collaboration can still happen without jeopardising sensitive company data.

Key Takeaways

1. Determine the tasks you want your members to do and assign them owner or member roles
2. For external Team members, determine what resources they will need access to and assign access accordingly
3. Ensure you have more than one Team Owner per Team
4. Ensure that your Team Owners are aware of their additional responsibilities in adding new Team members or creating and deleting Teams.

End of Chapter Checklist

o As a Team, decide on the settings that will create a safe and productive space for collaboration and coordination to occur

o Note your decisions down in the 10Ps workbook.

PERFORMANCE

When it comes to discussions about teams, the word "performance" often comes up. In this chapter, we will explore what performance means when it comes to working together and collaborating on a project. Specifically, we will look at ways to measure it so that you can keep on the right track to achieve your business outcomes. After all, that's what it's about.

In this hectic world of work, improving performance is an important and critical issue for many organisations. Many workers are not strangers to the "do more with less" mantra that their employers repeatedly recount at team meetings and briefings. They may have been at the receiving end of activities that build more efficiency into their departments, such as streamlining of processes, cost-cutting exercises, or restructure and redundancy programs to increase productivity and build scale across operations, but at what cost?

Businesses today are facing completely new challenges where strategies like those mentioned above may not ultimately result in the efficiencies they believe would happen. Simply put, change is too fast, too ambiguous, and too complex. It's also unpredictable. With unpredictable change, you cannot plan or prepare for what comes next because you don't know what comes next.

Businesses need to reframe how managers and leaders view work, and what and how teams and individuals perform their work—and interact with each other—to be able to manage and navigate this volatility.

In this chapter, we will explore what performance means and how you measure it and set up your team in Microsoft Teams for success.

What Is Performance?

In *Training Ain't Performance*, performance is defined as "a function of both behaviour and accomplishment of a person or a group of people. Performance includes the actions of a person and the result of the action or actions." (Stolovich, 2004).

What this means is that performance is both a behaviour to be displayed but also an accomplishment or outcome to be achieved. It is not about the technology you are using, nor about any solutions you are proposing.

It's also not defined as the number of people using Microsoft Teams, the number of "likes" on comments of your post, or even how many followers you have on your enterprise social networks. Performance goes far deeper than that. It's about applying practices that help us to achieve an outcome through people.

What Is Your Team's Role in Performance?

Your goal in your team is to help your fellow team members achieve the desired results and outcomes that help support the strategy of the business and to do so together, especially when there are factors such as dwindling resources, external market pressures, or financial constraints that constantly impact your team.

Internally, the team may be under pressure due to a lack of information and resources for their team project; have various demands on their job, such as time, attention, and focus; or be working in an environment where the organisational culture or climate is not conducive to being supportive. As a result, the performance of the team will be impacted if you're not aware of all the internal and external forces at play.

When the time comes to determine how your team will perform, you will need to revisit the problem you are trying to solve, which was covered earlier on in this book.

Where Are You Today and Where Do You Want to Be Tomorrow?

Firstly, you need to revisit the problem you are trying to solve, which we covered in the "Problem" chapter, as this will be your ultimate starting point. As an example, it can be anything from:

- How does your organisation find information quickly?
- How do you share knowledge or best practices across your networks?
- How do you solve a business problem?

- How do you manage exceptions?
- How do you work across departments?

Secondly, you need to analyse your current team's performance in relation to that problem, meaning you need to look at where you are today as a team and how ready you are to solve that problem. You may ask the following questions as a starting point:

- What is happening today that we don't want to happen?
- Why is it a problem for us?
- What are we doing today that we could be doing better/more effectively?
- What is the actual performance at issue?

Thirdly, you are now ready to envision a future state or the desired performance. Questions you may ask as a team are:

- What would we like to happen?
- What should we be doing?
- What is the desired performance?

Between your current and future state, you are now able to identify the gaps and define these as performance outcomes.

To make things easier for you, start from how much this problem and your current performance is costing you every year. If you put some tangible measure such as a dollar value on it, then you're more likely to sit up and take notice. "Hey, because we email all ten team members the updated reports, if they respond to my email and CC others, my inbox explodes. I spend a few hours every morning just going through it. What's it costing the business for me to be doing this?"

What Do Team Performance Outcomes Look Like?

Your team will need to define achievable performance outcomes that are specific, tangible, and, most of all, measurable against the overall business strategy.

Performance outcomes can be around different key areas, but as a starting point, you can consider the following as a suggestion. You may have others that are more relevant for your team, business, or organisation:

- **Customer**: what are some performance outcomes related to improving our customer experience or the way we work with them?
- **Financial**: what are some financial targets or goals that we can put in place to show improvement over time?
- **Business Processes:** what can we streamline, automate, or impact to improve the processes of delivery to our customers?
- **Innovation and Insights**: how will we measure new insights and innovation that continue to create value for customers and stakeholders?

Together with your team, you can now delve into the details and create specific performance outcomes for your Team. You may also call these KPIs, or Key Performance Indicators. Some examples are:

- Shave 10% off our operating costs within the next financial year
- Decrease the amount of workplace accidents by 20% in the next 12 months
- Reduce the amount of emails by 45% in the next six months
- Decrease the time it takes to fill in forms by 50% by identifying new automated workflows that will save the company $50,000 by the end of 2020.

Once your team decides on the performance outcomes, you will need to consider how you're going to track and measure the results. For example, you may decide to use some of the analytics within Power BI. Ultimately, you will need to consider ways to track against performance outcomes so that you can see trends over time.

Measuring Performance Outcomes

One of the leading pieces of research when it comes to measuring and assessing value creation in communities is the conceptual framework of value. In the model, Wenger, Trayner, and de Laat (2011) suggest the following five ways to measure value.

How Is Immediate Value Realised in the Team Itself?

This is seen by measuring the level of engagement, the number of interactions, and the levels of participation. To some, this may be known as "vanity metrics."

It is not an ideal way of measuring value, but it does provide some instant numbers for how people are interacting within Microsoft Teams. We wouldn't recommend using these vanity metrics as a way of measuring the success of your Team's implementation, because they offer no actual evidence of a business improvement. They're nice to know and make you feel good about the numbers of "likes" but, overall, they're meaningless.

More meaningful insights can be captured using third-party tools like Swoop for Teams (https://www.swoopanalytics.com/products/swoop-for-microsoft-teams/) or tyGraph Teams Analytics (https://tygraph.com/tygraph-for-microsoft-teams/). Tools such as these provide insights beyond just how many people are using your Team and, more importantly, how people interact within and across Teams to create connections, breaking down silos within your organisation.

How Is the Team's Potential Value Realised?

In this, you can measure potential value through outcomes such as an increase in Team members' new skills or capabilities, or in the understanding and education of new tools used by the team that generated new learning of their applications.

How Is the Applied Value of the Team Realised?

Applied value refers to the adaptation and application of the team to a specific situation, for example, based on the conversations and the teamwork experience in Microsoft Teams, what was created, used, or changed as a result. It could be identifying a new association or partnership between business units or creating a new product or service for your customers.

Applied value relates to leveraging the knowledge that was shared in the Team through application to some business issue, project, or need. Alternatively, it could mean the establishment of a new practice. By demonstrating your Team's applied value, you're able to promote and showcase a success story to your managers and leaders about how teamwork within Microsoft Teams generated business outcomes. These are the stories that people will want to hear. It makes the use of Microsoft Teams relevant and meaningful for them because they can now see the applications.

How Is the Value of the Team Realised?

So, you've changed your team's practice by moving from email to Microsoft Teams. You've shown some applications of how they can create or refine new ways of working. How is their new knowledge impacting business strategy and outcomes?

How Is the Value Reframed?

In this last phase, value is reframed and redefined. It is a reconsideration of value and the proposing of new models and frameworks that may require "re-negotiations with the powers-that-be who have the legitimacy to define success at these levels."

What this means is that your team has redefined the way work and teamwork are conducted in your organisation and may have come across processes or ways of work that are now considered redundant or too traditional to work in a modern workplace.

Reframing value may result in a new vision, sets of expectations, and frameworks emerging that will need new discussions and strategies.

In summary, "Performance" relates to the specific goals your Team will accomplish. They are written in such a way that they can be measured and evaluated against bigger goals, such as organisational or business strategy.

Devising goals aligned to strategy enables your team to best promote and link their Team actions to how they've directly created value for the organisation and its clients or community.

Key Takeaways

1. Undertake an analysis of where you are today versus where you want to be tomorrow
2. Identify the performance gaps that need to be closed

3. Decide on the performance outcomes you would like to achieve in a specific manner and how to measure them.

End of Chapter Checklist

○ Document what success looks like and how you will measure that success in your 10Ps workbook.

PROVISIONING

We are sorry to say that this part of the 10Ps may be the most frustrating for you. Or, it may be your favourite aspect of getting your team up and running on Microsoft Teams…depending on which organisation you work for. Provisioning is the one area where we consistently see inconsistency across our customers.

In some organisations, you will have complete control of what Teams you create, when you create them, and how you manage them to achieve your business objectives. You are trusted to create your own collaboration and coordination spaces just like you create your own Word documents and Excel spreadsheets. Your Information Technology team is just delivering you a service, and as the subject matter expert in your area, you are empowered to use that service as you see fit to help you achieve your goals.

In other organisations, to get a Team created you might have to fill in an e-Form, get approval from your manager, then sacrifice your first-born child to someone in IT before they deem your request worthy of a Team. Structures are put in place to restrict or even discourage you from creating a Team. In fact, in one example, we saw an IT team put a convoluted request and approval process in place simply so they could cross-charge a business unit for delivering the service.

Processes like this, while annoying and universal in their ability to slow things down (just when you have the momentum and want to start things yesterday!) are workable if you understand the process and the timeframes involved.

However, if you are in the unlucky minority, even sacrificing two children, sending a gift basket and organising four tickets for the game on Friday night to "Brad on the Service Desk" may not be enough. In some organisations, your IT team may have established a position to lock down Team (and Office 365 Group) creation to such a degree that no matter how many favours you ask of your CIO, you simply won't be able to create a Team.

For those of you working in organisations with this "significant" or "overreaching" governance in place, while this chapter may not be as relevant today, the ideas we discuss over the next few pages may help you start a conversation with your IT team to reach a more pragmatic or business outcome-focused position. Generally, "lock everything down" is the default response when a new technology and its business application are not entirely understood.

Guess what? You can help the IT team gain that understanding.

Armed with examples and specific ideas of how you want to use Microsoft Teams (all detailed using the 10Ps framework), you may find that your IT team will loosen up some of the restrictions on self-service or demand-led creation of collaboration and coordination spaces using Microsoft Teams.

For those of you who can create Teams today...breathe a sigh of relief!

Seriously, though, this chapter will introduce you to some advanced provisioning ideas you may not be aware of, which may transform how you think about the role Microsoft Teams plays in project or committee initiation, emergency management or disaster recovery, and any other scenario where you may use similar Team structures across your organisation. Ironically, it will mean you might want to work with IT to make this work for you. This time, however, it probably will not require any type of ritualistic sacrifice.

So...What Is Provisioning?

Simply put, provisioning is the process of setting up your Microsoft Teams Team. In smaller organisations, provisioning may simply mean, "Click on 'Join or create a team'," then following the bouncing ball through the new Team creation process. In larger organisations, there will be rules, policies, and architectural decisions that mean it may not be as simple as a few clicks.

Let's break provisioning down into four broad buckets:

- Doing it yourself
- Receiving assistance from the IT team
- Using templates
- Automating what goes into your Team.

Creating a Team — Do It Yourself

Assuming you work in an organisation that has empowered you to create your own Teams, creating a Team is relatively simple.

1. Open up Microsoft Teams
2. Click on "Join or create a Team"
3. Click on "Create a Team"
4. Click on "Build a Team from scratch"
5. Select the kind of Team it will be (private or public)
6. Give your Team a name and description
7. Add members to your Team
8. Add some channels
9. Get to work!

Wait...hold on a minute. You didn't just go and create a Team, did you? Yes, it is simple to create a Team. However, before you dive in and create your Team, you should spend a few minutes thinking *about* your Team.

Use the 10Ps framework (which we discuss in this book) to guide you through your thought process.

- **Problem**: are we solving a problem by creating this Team? If not, you probably don't need to create it.
- **Purpose**: do we have a clear purpose? If so, does the name of this Team make that purpose clear?
- **People**: who do we need in this Team? Are there subsets of people which mean we should break this into two different Teams, or use private channels? Will there be guests from outside of our organisation?

- **Priorities**: what are the 3–7 things we are going to focus on in this Team? Do they map nicely to channels?
- **Principles**: how are we going to agree to use this Team? What does a like or a mention mean?
- **Plugins**: what third-party applications or websites might we want to include in the Team, so we don't need to switch to other windows all the time?
- **Permissions**: who should be able to do what in this Team? Should it be private, or should we encourage others to join?
- **Performance**: what does success look like?
- **Provisioning**: umm…this is meta. Let's assume create it yourself for now :)
- **Perishability**: how long will this Team last? What will we do when we are finished with it?

Once you have considered all of these factors and are comfortable that the design of your new Team will meet your collaboration or coordination needs…then go ahead and start creating.

Remember that just because you have the power to create Teams, it doesn't mean that you should create as many Teams as possible. Use the 10Ps framework to determine what Teams you should create and how you should set them up. Documenting your answers to each of the 10Ps before you start will enable you to create collaboration and coordination spaces in Microsoft Teams that are fit for purpose and don't raise suspicion or eyebrows from IT, who deep down fear having to clean up "Teams sprawl."

Creating a Team — Assisted by the IT Team

Many of you reading this book will only be able to create a Team through a process established by your IT team. Despite the *slight* sarcasm earlier in this chapter, we understand that organisations have some good reasons for putting a small level of governance around the Team creation and provisioning process. Usually, it's to ensure that:

- Duplicate Teams are minimised as much as possible
- Only people in the marketing team create Teams that have the word "Marketing" in their name
- Teams which have external guests always have the prefix [EXT] or [External] at the start of the Team name
- Discovering related Teams is easy
- There are two group owners, just in case one of you moves on
- They can cross-charge your business unit (*not a good reason!*).

In every organisation, the process will be slightly different. You can expect to provide some information about the Team you want prior to it being created for you by the IT team. Try to be as descriptive as possible when filling in the form. You can use your responses to each of the 10Ps to help the service desk (or your manager, if they need to approve your request) to understand what you are trying to achieve.

Depending on how things are set up, the creation of the Team could still happen instantly if your organisation uses some special Microsoft Teams governance or provisioning software, or it may need a review by someone in IT. In most cases, the process should only take a day or two, maximum. However, if you know that process takes a little bit longer in your organisation, make sure you plan and request your Team earlier than you need it.

Creating a Team — Using Templates

If your IT team has already worked with others in your organisation, they may have created several templates to help you get started with Microsoft Teams.

For example, if you want to create a Team to manage a formal committee meeting, there may already be an approved Team template developed by your executive support officers, governance team, or company secretary that meets your compliance requirements and includes the appropriate channels so you can get started straight away. Another example could be a template that includes all the channels aligned to your Project Management methodology, approved by your Project Management Office.

Generally, templates will only be available via an IT-assisted provisioning process. They may be displayed as options on your "Teams request form." Or you may need to call your service desk directly to see what templates are available. If in doubt, get in touch with IT to discuss it.

If you have created a Team and you want to create another that is similar, it might be a good candidate to turn into a template and make available to others in your organisation. If so, make sure you bring it to the attention of your IT team. You can not only save yourself time but also make the lessons you have learned available to others in your organisation.

Creating a Team — Automating What Goes into Your Team

If you are a member of the Project Management Office and regularly work on projects, run a bid management team, or have a high volume of Teams that are consistent (for example, a Team for every class at your university), this approach to provisioning will excite you.

Imagine a world where, when your project was approved, you kicked off your bid, or when a class was finalised at the start of a semester and a collaboration and coordination space was created for you in Microsoft Teams. Automatically. Without having to ask someone for it. Then imagine if that Team:

- Was named to clearly demonstrate the purpose of the Team
- Was built with the right channels in place, per your regular Team template

- Was populated with all the project initiation documents, your tender response templates or course overview documents, using data from your project approval, customer relationship management, or student management systems
- Had the right people added with the right owner/member permissions

…just a few seconds after the approval to start on the project or work on the bid was given.

Now, this isn't something that most people reading this book will be able to do themselves. However, it's important to know that it is possible. If there is repeatability in your work, and you are currently spending hours a week creating documentation and setting up Teams to meet your needs, we encourage you to have a discussion with your IT team. They may be able to assist you in automating some or all those processes. Just ask them this one question:

- "I am interested in automating some of our Team creation processes. I've heard of something called the 'Graph API' which we could use to automate the set-up of our Teams. Then we could use 'Power Automate (Flow)' or an 'Azure Run Book' to put the right documents into the right channels. Who can I talk to about this?"

If your IT team doesn't have the expertise internally but it makes financial sense for you to automate Team creation, you could potentially work with a Microsoft Partner and your IT team to make it a possibility.

What Is the Best Provisioning Approach?

Simple. The best provisioning approach is the one that takes you the least amount of time, considering the rules and policies that have been put in place by your IT team. For ad-hoc or reasonably unique use cases, creating your Team yourself or using the IT-assisted process (if it exists in your organisation) is the way to go.

If you are going to create multiple Teams with very similar structures, start out by creating them yourself. Test them in the real world in real situations. Only once you have created your first few Teams and are comfortable with the naming approach, the channel structure, etc., should you consider starting to template or automate. The upside of templates or automation is huge, but it is only huge if you are templating or automating the right things! Start slow, get it right, then start working with your IT team or Microsoft Partner to engineer the perfect Teams provisioning process for you.

Key Takeaways

1. Don't just create a Team; have a think about what you want to create first, using the 10Ps framework as a guide
2. Make sure you understand the specific provisioning process for your organisation, as every IT team treats provisioning a little bit differently

3. If you are thinking about automation, take it slow: get your Team design and structure right before templating and automating Team creation.

End of Chapter Checklist

o Document how you will provision your Team in your 10Ps workbook
o Create your Team using the method most appropriate for your organisation (do it yourself or IT-assisted), put it into practice, and then decide if it makes sense to template or automate.

PERISHABILITY

"When you're dealing with a team this size, it's like herding cats," said the Royal Australian Navy captain, standing at the front of a packed lecture theatre.

Around him, sitting or standing wherever there was room, were men and women, officers and sailors, from all around the world. They had come to listen to the final and the most critical phase—the debrief—of one of the Australian Navy's important exercises for the year, *Exercise Pacific Reach*.

It was 2007, and I was a lieutenant commander sitting in that audience. To my right was one of my peers, senior to me, who had many years of operational experience. To my left was a lieutenant from the Italian Navy, who, during the exercise, had become a good friend—possibly because I heartily exclaimed "Una fascia, una razza!" in the ship's wardroom one night to explain the exercise that we were all in.

One face. One race. That's what teamwork is about. *Exercise Pacific Reach* is an international navy exercise held every three years that tests the skills and capabilities of submarine escape and rescue. For one week, differences are set aside, and participating navies collaborate on and coordinate simulated operations for searching and finding missing submarines and for rescuing the personnel that may be trapped within them.

I had submitted my leave from my corporate day job as a learning and development consultant in a large bank to participate in the exercise in Perth, Western Australia, as the public relations officer. For the week of the seagoing phase of the exercise, my role involved daily briefings at the Exercise Command Headquarters to understand the various activities during the day and night that involved helicopter, ship, or submarine movements.

It was my responsibility to work with and escort the news media teams and get them out to the various activities at sea so that they could capture the best stories and visual imagery to be published on national news that night. I was also responsible for briefing senior officers on talking points for their interviews on camera. With a small team of videographers and photographers, we boarded and disembarked various international ships, helicopters, zodiac boats, and other watercraft to speak to the people participating in the exercise and to get the best story and photos for Defence media.

In the lecture theatre, the captain continued his introduction to the debrief phase of the exercise by showing an amusing short video of cowboys herding cats before delving into the main presentation and inviting other people to the stage to present their findings.

The debrief took several hours, but the individual navies and teams who participated in the exercise had already had their debriefs and slowly closed their teams down. This was the last gathering before the big goodbye BBQ.

People were now looking forward to the beginning of a new week. Some were going back home to loved ones.

Others were posted to a new ship or a new shore role. Others, like me, were going back to their real life in the corporate world.

That's when the tiredness and exhaustion descended on me, but there was something else, too. There was the feeling of sadness and mourning.

An ending.

My life for one week was put on hold, as all my time, energy and focus centred on contributing to and participating in this team effort. The people who were part of the exercise made it, and over the long days and nights, I made some great friendships and rekindled some old ones.

There were some tough times, when I was mentally and physically exhausted, wondering why I accepted such a challenge and cursing myself for doing so. However, there were also other times, such as the quiet early morning conversations over a hot brew with the pilot in the helo ops centre on the flight deck, that made it worthwhile.

Being part of this exercise made me realise the importance of teamwork. Sitting in the lecture theatre with my peers from around the world made me realise that teams, sadly, have an end date, an expiry, an ending.

Back in 1965, Bruce Tuckman developed one of the most well-known and influential models of group development. You may know it as the Forming—Storming—Norming—Performing model. Some ten years later, he added a fifth stage called Adjourning.

In my experience, this final stage is usually incomplete or not conducted at all. In fact, I struggle to think of any time during my corporate career that any focus or attention was placed on this phase. Too often, we were assigned to the next project to start the lifecycle all over again.

Adjourning your project must have the same level of interest as the other phases. As your Team's project comes to an end, your Team members will experience a sense of loss, and it's important to recognise this feeling and end the project on a positive note.

It's time to celebrate the hard work of people in the Team and the lessons learned and to reflect on what could be improved in the future.

It's also a time to consider and finalise what happens to all the content sitting within the channels of your Team. Should you keep it visible? Should you archive it? Should you upload it to your records management system?

This is the last phase of the 10Ps framework, in which you consider your Team's perishability.

Coming to the End of Your Team Lifecycle

Contrary to belief, it's best to start with the end in mind. Rather than wait until your Team has run its course and then make decisions, we recommend that you consider this phase up front and early on in your implementation. Why?

Many of the Team members will have been reassigned to new projects, and their focus and attention will be drawn away to new and more exciting Teams. It is easier to determine and decide the rules and actions that your team needs to close out your Team, well before the end.

This is where you decide what the end of your Team's life looks like, and it's a great starting point. Some of the questions you will need to decide as a Team are:

- When do we determine that the Team has run its course, and what does this look like? (For example, is it an end date, an action, an activity, or simply no additional conversations being added to it?)
- How will we capture the lessons learned from our teamwork so that they can be reused and shared with others in our organisation who may need these to consider for their own teams and projects?
- Who needs to know that the Team will be closing? (for example, stakeholders, managers, leaders, business?), and will they be required to have access to any of the information or content within it?
- How will we share and communicate the closure of our Team to others?
- What will happen to the content, data, and information held within the Team?
- Are there any specific expiration and retention policies we will need to follow?
- How will we determine when we need to archive a Team versus delete a Team?

Critical Reflection in the Workplace

Rigg and Trehan (2008) argue in "*Critical Reflection in the Workplace: Is It Just Too Difficult?*" that reflection has been criticised by workplaces in the past for being too individualised and focused on personal growth and development.

Organisations must consider what they term "critical reflection" as "the process by which adults identify the assumptions governing their actions, locate the historical and cultural origins of the assumptions, question the meaning of the assumptions, and develop alternative ways of acting."

Critical reflection as a team allows us to translate and interpret the way our team worked together to create new knowledge, behaviours, and actions from "ordinary and extraordinary experiences." So, how can you do this for your own team?

Creating a "Lessons Learned" Channel in Your Team

Where appropriate, we recommend setting up a channel in your Team to capture moments that could be used as potential learning experiences and to encourage everyone to capture these as they happen.

These could be situations where the team faltered, a goal failed to be achieved, the team had some difficulty, or it was challenged in some way that created tension. You can even add moments when the Team was working well.

You can call it anything you like—"What I Learned Today," "What Have I Learned," but the important thing is to encourage everyone to share their lessons and then conduct a team debrief or review of these at the end of your project.

An alternative to a Lessons Learned channel may be to add a Microsoft Forms tab to your General channel. The form can include simple questions that will help you to capture lessons or stories which could be used to aid learning in the future.

What Questions Can You Ask During Your Debrief?

Too often, end of project debriefs don't occur, and as a result there may be a missed opportunity for understanding the factors at play and how you can prepare yourself for future team projects.

Brookfield (1988) outlines the following model for conducting critical reflections:

1. Assumption analysis
2. Contextual awareness
3. Imaginative speculation
4. Reflective scepticism

As part of the perishability phase of your Team, you will need to consider reflecting on the project and asking some questions that may not have clear answers. Some members may not be comfortable sharing in depth as it may touch on some organisational and cultural aspects of how work is done in the company.

Using Brookfield's model, we can apply some questions to ask during this perishability phase, specifically to allow us to learn deep lessons that challenge our assumptions, encourage new knowledge to be assimilated, and build new behaviours for the future.

You can ask:

- What were our team's assumptions of how we worked together and collaborated within that Team and as a Team?
- What was our team's awareness of the context in which we were working (the environment, resources, conditions, operations, culture, sensitivities)?
- How could we imagine and speculate on a new way of working and thinking so that that we challenge our own way of working for our next Team project?
- How can we question everything above so that we can draw new insights and perspectives from the trends and patterns we saw?

Capture Personal Reflections and Stories

When employees complete their teamwork projects or move onto others in their organisation, or if they leave their employment, the cost of lost knowledge to the organisation can be immense.

The corporate knowledge to which we are referring is an employee's "tacit knowledge." That is, the knowledge that resides in your employees' heads, which can be defined as "skills and experiences that people have but are not codified and may not necessarily be expressed." (Chugh, 2015). Tacit knowledge can be described in different ways:

- Knowing how to do something rather than knowing what

- Expressing and interacting in different ways
- Learning through observation, role modelling, and practice
- Acquiring knowledge through experimentation and experience
- Learning by intuition.

One of the ways to capture the tacit knowledge that sits in the heads of your team members is to capture their stories and experiences of working in that team. This way, the tacit knowledge becomes explicit, and is written down or expressed in some form through which it can be transferred to others.

What Are Some Ways to Capture the Knowledge of Your Team Members?

Luckily, within the various Microsoft suite of products, there are a multitude of ways to capture the knowledge of your Team members. We will provide some examples to get you started and get you thinking about how to use the stories of Team members to share success with others within the Team, other employees in the company, and other people outside your organisation.

This process is what you may already understand as "using the inner and outer loop" to share information.

Capturing Knowledge Within the Team (Inner Loop)

The inner loop refers to the knowledge that is captured by Team members, for Team members. You can capture this in various ways:

- **Record all virtual Team meetings within relevant channels** so that they are accessible to others when needed. Use the chat for the Team to capture ideas as they occur and to ensure the conversation keeps going long after the meeting.
- **Create "The Week That Was,"** a summary of key Team project and learning outcomes that happened in that week. This could be posted into the General channel to consolidate all the key activities that occurred across your Team that week.
- **Create a Big Questions/What Is Broken channel in your Team** where big ideas, hairy questions, or issues that require more time for collective reflection and planning are posted. This way, the conversation around these cannot be lost within the main conversation.
- **Encourage your team members to capture their thoughts** in other ways, such as writing blog posts or creating video updates of what they're doing.
- **Encourage your team members to update their Yammer profiles with any new skills, capabilities, or experiences they've picked up** along the way on the project as this will build upon their career development and project expertise.

Once this knowledge is captured, it will be specific to that Team and project. When the time comes to archive this Team according to your IT policy, this is where you will need to have a more long-term view of how that knowledge will be shared.

This is where your post-team debrief will come into play. You will use the stories and key lessons learned during the debrief to create stories that will be shared to the outer loop.

That is, by moving these lessons to the outer loop, you ensure that these stories are discoverable by others across your organisation.

Sharing Your Knowledge to the Outer Loop

This is where you can be creative in sharing key lessons and success stories through different methods and media across your organisation. Use the various Microsoft 365 products at your fingertips to present information in different ways. For example:

- **Create a "Today I Learned" community in Yammer**: encourage your Team members to share their "a-ha" moments in a community for others to view and learn from. Why not include a specific hashtag of your project so that these stories are discoverable?
- **Share a news article outlining your key lessons on a SharePoint communication site**: document and synthesise what you learned into a formal article that others can learn from in the future.

- **Create a co-created video of your team's reflections** of working on that Team and share it on Stream, Yammer, or your intranet. Encourage conversations by asking others for their input.
- **Capture key lessons as part of a slideshow presentation on PowerPoint** and share it on Yammer.
- **Encourage team members to be speakers at organisational or internal department team events** such as team meetings, project briefings, or departmental committee meetings.
- **Conduct an Hour of Power** in which any one of your team members can conduct an hour-long webinar with an open invitation across the organisation on a skill, experience, or lesson learned during the teamwork collaboration. This is what is known as social learning: people learning from each other and with each other.

There are many more ways to share lessons learned and success stories, and we encourage you to be creative here as you're the best person to know how your organisation will receive and value this information.

But what about people and networks outside of your company? Think of this as the open network: everything that sits outside of the organisation's walls.

Sharing Your Knowledge Outside the Organisation

Assuming there is nothing private, sensitive, or confidential to share, such as customer names and details, this is where we interact with our peers from the same and even different industries. This type of sharing is for building networks, having conversations and sharing insights.

Some organisations may have strict guidelines regarding their employees sharing information to social networks, so we encourage you to find out what these are and abide by them. Here are some ways in which you can share what you learned on your project to people outside your organisation:

Blog Posts

- Write a reflective blog post and share that to your social networks
- Write a collaborative team blog post about your experiences

Tweets

- Share tweets of key lessons learned using a specific hashtag
- Create a Tweet chat where you encourage others in your network to share their lessons learned from similar projects

Articles

- Write an article that can be shared on your website
- Pitch an article to a corporate newsletter or trade magazine

LinkedIn

- Share key lessons learned in LinkedIn posts or write a LinkedIn article
- Update your LinkedIn profile with any new skills, experiences, projects, and capabilities learned on that Team project
- Do a LinkedIn Live video interview with key team members and have them share key points of the project and what they would do differently
- Create an infographic of tips and tricks learned that you could share freely and start conversations

Videos

- Create a video of key lessons and share on your preferred social network
- Create a story around your project so that you can present it at industry conferences and events
- Conduct a behind-the-scenes video tour and interviews of all the team members to ascertain what they learned

Presentations

- Create a SlideShare presentation of what you learned on the Team.

Celebrate!

By now, you're probably thinking that to wind down a Team, it seems like there's more work! That's true to some extent, so let's turn our attention to what you really want to read about...the celebration!

As mentioned, the adjournment of the team means some form of goodbye, so that team members can bring some closure to their work and the bonds created in the Team.

Celebrating the team can be done in any way, and really, you're going to be the experts here. You don't need us to tell you this.

It's likely that you've probably already talked about what this may be, such as a lunch at a nearby pizza restaurant or a morning tea (and yes, you can even do these virtually!).

Regardless of how you choose to celebrate the Team's close, there's still one or two tasks left to finish.

It's Not Over Until...

You've conducted your debriefs, you've shared your lessons and stories with the organisation and the world, you've had your goodbye lunch and reflected on how this teamwork collaboration has supported you in your role, and you're looking forward to your next team project. What's left to be done?

Here, the Team Owners and IT administrators are responsible for deciding how to archive and store the Team information.

Your IT or Records Management team may have specific policies around what happens to Teams at the end of their project lifecycle. They may archive the Team, or they may delete it.

IMPORTANT: deleting a Team will mean that all associated channels, files, and chats are deleted. You will never be able to access any information within this Team again.

The alternative is to archive a Team. Archiving means that all activity in that Team will cease; however, you and Team owners will still be able to add or remove members and update roles. You can also choose to make the Team read-only in SharePoint as another option. In future, if you need to un-archive the Team, you can do so, and you will have the Team back up and running again. This is particularly handy if you run events every year, and you want to refer back to what you did last year or the year before.

We encourage you to archive your Team first at the end of your project to ensure that no information is lost. This way, should you need it again, it can be reactivated. Remember, if you delete your Team, all information will be lost.

Speak to your IT or Records Management team regarding the best action here as they may have archival and retention policies that you are not aware of.

Summary

The perishability of a Team is a principle that is just as critical as the others in the framework when it comes to determining the structure of your Team.

Consider it not as an ending but as a new beginning for your Team members; they have contributed and participated in an experience in which they solved a problem together and had an opportunity to learn from and with each other in the process.

Using Microsoft Teams enables your Team members to express their ideas, knowledge, insights, and experiences in different ways and methods using the various Microsoft products, tools, and plugins. This, in turn, encourages conversations across their team, department, organisation, and maybe even the world.

Don't think of your Team's perishability like herding cats, as the Navy officer did at the beginning of this chapter. It might have been like this in the days of email and email threads, but with Microsoft Teams, you now have an opportunity to capture the unique insights and experiences of your Team members, and these will have a direct and positive impact on not only the individual but also on your organisation itself.

Key Takeaways

1. Capture the personal stories and key lessons learned in a number of different ways so that they can be shared to your organisations, customers, and stakeholders
2. Decide how you will archive information and files in Teams. You may need to seek advice from your IT department or someone involved with how information is stored and managed in your organisation
3. Remember to celebrate!

End of Chapter Checklist

o   Document how you will capture and share the lessons learned from your Team in your 10Ps workbook

o   If you haven't already—it is time to create your Team!

PART THREE

PATTERNS FROM THE REAL WORLD

N ow that you have the 10Ps framework to help structure the way you and your team use Microsoft Teams, let's look for some inspiration to help you get started. We will explore a selection of real-world Microsoft Teams patterns, examples—structured using the 10Ps framework—that you could use straight away with your team or use as a starting point to structure Microsoft Teams to work for you.

You could start with every team at your organisation and make decisions based on the 10Ps framework. However, you would soon notice that many Teams are set up in much the same way. While not every organisation standardises teamwork to the level of a fast food chain, it makes sense to set up replicable structures to scale out a business.

Just as teams within an organisation are somewhat similar, the same can be said across *Adopt & Embrace*'s diverse range of customers. It is almost unheard of to find a team that cannot learn something from the experience of another Team at another organisation, even if they are in different industries or functions.

The idea for Microsoft Teams patterns was initially inspired by some well-known software engineering theory that dates to the 1970s. A "design pattern" was a reusable strategy to solve a common problem. The problems are generic, and the solutions are necessarily conceptual. A design pattern is a guide, but the actual software implementation could be written in almost any programming language. It is the high-level, strategic nature of the approach which has kept the design pattern approach alive to this day. Patterns don't become outdated, even though programming languages come and go.

The trick with the pattern approach is to be able to recognise which pattern(s) are applicable. Most real-world problems will have elements of multiple patterns, but typically only one will be the "real" problem that needs solving. It's sometimes not obvious which is the dominant issue and which is an unwelcome distraction.

In the following examples, we have not only synthesised common problems but have provided reusable strategies to address those problems by referring back to our 10Ps framework.

EXPERT COMMUNITY OF PRACTICE

Problem

Over the next few years, our organisation will experience an immense transition period as it upgrades systems and technologies to the cloud and automates workflows for some of our departments, such as the contact centre. With intense competition in the marketplace, we need our workforce to be flexible and navigate these constant changes but, at the same time, see opportunities where others don't.

This will require our people to have new skills and capabilities that they may not currently possess in order to build insight and intelligence into our workplace. We understand that they have knowledge, skills, and capabilities that may not have been identified or acknowledged by our organisational systems.

We want to identify these people and provide them with a voice through which they can share their knowledge and expertise with others and, in the process, learn new things that may support them in identifying new opportunities inside or outside our company.

The problem is that we need new and innovative ideas for products to ensure our position in the marketplace remains competitive; we have smart people, but we don't know who they are or what they can help us with. We need to identify our talent and then match this talent with others so that they can play an active role in the development of new products and services to cater for our ever-changing marketplace.

Purpose

We want to build a culture of knowledge and capability-building through people sharing their insights and expertise with peers across the organisation. In particular, the purpose of the Team is to showcase new ideas and insights so that new innovations may be identified by the community that the organisation can use as pilot test products.

The purpose of our Team is to provide an online Team space where people who have interest, motivation, and expertise can show and share their work, share their knowledge and practices, collaborate on joint projects, and find mutual areas of project work around solving complex organisational problems in a co-operative manner supported by their managers.

The name of this Team will be: Transformation Community of Practice.

People

The people involved in this Team will:

- Be volunteers
- Have an interest in sharing knowledge around a theme or topic (e.g. drone technology, artificial intelligence, coding, and other topics that the team identifies as skill gaps)
- Come from all parts of our national business.

Priorities

- **Define**: define the need for open and transparent work practices and acknowledge that our people have unique skills and capabilities that may remain hidden. Bring these hidden skills to the surface so that our organisation may find pockets of expertise across the national business; allow our people to connect and network with each other; highlight opportunities for co-operation and collaboration.
- **Promote**: promote the public Team to the organisation for people to join in the pilot and be aware of the value and benefits of transparent work and learning practices, for the purpose of identifying opportunities to collaborate on new work projects and initiatives identified within the Team.
- **Evaluate**: define some initial success measures for the pilot Team.

- **Select**: select some initial advocates who may act as role models and influencers in the business for this community; seek feedback on how they would inspire collaboration and promote transparent work practices in the Team.
- **Build**: build the Team with the advocates for Working Out Loud.
- **Launch**: launch the Team and pilot for six months; measure against success criteria.
- **Determine how to scale**: based on the results of the pilot, determine how to build and scale other communities of practices around new skills and capabilities needed in the business to face the future.

It is anticipated that the following channels be created around the above priorities:

- General
- Design and Development
- Evaluation Criteria
- Pilot Group
- Promotion
- Build
- Launch.

Principles

- No emails will be sent to Team members—all emails to be placed into the relevant channel
- The General channel will be reserved for Team-wide communication only

- Direct messages will only be used for one-to-one communications that are not relevant to the wider group
- Team members commit to sharing valuable and thoughtful posts, helping other Team members by linking to the relevant resources
- Members are to set notifications so they follow the channel for any updates
- Team members will help each other through use of peer coaching and support, when and as required
- Team member managers will support use of Microsoft Teams and will allow time off to undertake development activities during working hours identified by the Team
- Team members will actively share their good ideas or tips on how to use Teams in a dedicated channel for this function so that peer learning is supported for the use of Microsoft Teams.

Plugins

The Team will require the following plugins or tabs:

- Wiki for a "Welcome to the Community of Practice Team" guide
- Microsoft Planner for members to assign tasks and activities
- Microsoft OneNote for collaborative notetaking and curating resources and links about the topic

- Microsoft Stream for access to recorded videos of meetings or guest speaker events; individual team member knowledge-sharing videos
- Microsoft Excel to capture details of development events that the team may hold.

Permissions

- Public Team where anyone may be encouraged to join
- Three Team owners identified
- External access provided on a case-by-case basis, as it's anticipated that the Teams may invite external guests as guest presenters to Team events; they will not need access to shared resources but will require a way to communicate one-to-one with Team members for a short period of time.

Performance

- Identify at least two new product innovations that can be tested for the market within three months of the Team being set up
- Reduce the amount of training spend due to peer learning and networking within the online communities.

Provisioning

- We will need the support of IT to show the team how to use Microsoft Teams to create Teams and edit settings initially; however, over time, we anticipate that this responsibility will be with selected Team owners who are comfortable with the process.

Perishability

- Team owners will archive the Team after no communication or engagement has occurred in over two years and will advise Team members of this.

GRADUATE INDUCTION AND ONBOARDING

Problem

Every year, every three months, our company must recruit, induct, train, and place 50 graduates across the business into different parts of our organisation. During their three-month rotations, graduates are expected to undertake development and networking opportunities that will help support their career. This also enables our managers and leaders to identify high potential and talent for permanent placements at the end of the 12 months.

This 12-month program requires a coordination effort by not only the Graduate Development team in Human Resources but also by our external agencies, such as recruitment and psychology services, and trainers and facilitators who conduct soft skills training. Our managers and leaders also need to have line of sight capacities over the progress of their graduates through the program.

Currently, this information resides in our file directory within folders in SharePoint. We have a SharePoint page—our intranet—which we update with information for graduates and managers. However, this is inaccessible to our external agents. Currently, much of our work and communication is done via email and team meetings. The problem is that as our graduate program is growing, we need a better way to plan, coordinate, and streamline our approach so that we can better serve our managers and partners as well as our company's future—the graduates.

Purpose

The purpose of this Team is to enable the Graduate Development team to coordinate recruitment, induction, development, and placement of graduates into the business for their 12-month graduate program.

The name of the Team will be: Graduate Development Program Australia.

People

- Graduate Development team in Human Resources
- External agents such as our recruitment partners, psychological services and training consultants and facilitators
- Selected business managers and leaders as Team members

Priorities

- Create the program design for the next 12 months

- Develop the recruiting strategy for the selection of recruitment partners who will assist in the grad program
- Develop assessment criteria for potential graduates with recruiters
- Undertake and develop the selection strategy and process of graduates in conjunction with recruiters and business managers
- Develop the onboarding activities that will occur throughout the program
- Develop the training strategy with selected external training facilitators and partners
- Develop coaching plans for graduates and communicate these to business managers
- Develop the workplace placement strategy and processes for graduate placement into business every three months
- Develop the transition to workforce strategy for selected graduates for full-time roles
- Develop outplacement strategy for unsuccessful graduates
- Develop an evaluation strategy to obtain feedback from all graduates, stakeholders, business managers and partners for improvement to the program next year
- Encourage Team to learn continuously through the program

It is anticipated that the following channels be created around the above priorities:

- General
- Program Design and Evaluation
- Recruitment and Assessment
- Onboarding
- Training and Coaching
- Workplace Placement
- Transition to Workplace
- Outplacement

Principles

- No emails will be sent to Team members, all emails to be placed into relevant channel
- The General channel will be reserved for Team-wide communication only
- Private 1:1 chat will only be used for one-to-one communications that are not relevant to the wider group
- Members will respond to posts where they are mentioned (@) by replying, liking, or mentioning others to keep the conversation going
- Team members will help each other through use of peer coaching and support when and as required
- Team member managers will support their use of Microsoft Teams and will allow time off to undertake development activities during working hours identified by the Team

Plugins

The team will require the following plugins:

- Wiki for "How to Use this Graduate Development Team" guide
- Access to Trello (our team uses Trello to assign tasks and activities with our external agencies; however, there's an internal project currently looking at how we can move our Trello activities to Microsoft Planner in the next few months)
- Access to the SharePoint document library for all Graduate Development files
- Access to Graduate Intranet page (a SharePoint Communication Site) where the team can update the rest of the organisation
- Microsoft Excel
- *Power Automate (Flow) (for discussion): explore the automation of our graduate enquiries email directly into Team channel for action (graduateenquiry@companyx.com.au)
- **Yammer (for discussion): explore opportunity to create an online space for current and ex-graduates to create a community for sharing knowledge and experiences of their workplace stories; this was based on graduate feedback from last year's survey that we would like to explore further
- No connectors or bots required.

Permissions

- Private Team where specific stakeholders will be encouraged to join
- Three Team owners identified from the current Graduate Development Team
- Guest access provided to our psychological services and recruitment services (private and confidential material will not be made available)
- Team member access to selected business managers and leaders.

Performance

- Reduce the amount of emails generated to plan and coordinate the yearly Graduate Development Program
- Reduce the time it takes to search for and place graduates into vacancies in the business every three months for their rotations
- Identify the highest calibre graduates for permanent placements at the end of 12 months
- Have one source of truth for accurate records of graduates and grant all the Team and our external parties access
- Streamline the process from the time it takes to source, identify, interview, recruit, place, and train new graduates
- Provide managers with current information about their new graduate placements every three months.

Provisioning

- The Graduate Program owner will work with the IT Service Desk to submit the appropriate paperwork to request the new Team to be created.

Perishability

- Team owners will archive the Team at the end of the program; however, it will not be deleted for five years so we can leverage the resources for upcoming graduate programs
- File management in accordance with our company IT policy for graduate details.

BUSINESS CONFERENCE PLANNING

Problem

Every year, Human Resources hosts, plans, and coordinates a one-day conference where key senior leaders from the business share their vision, strategy and plans for the business in that year. The conference is attended by all members of Human Resources and selected internal guests who are currently working with HR teams in their business.

Purpose

The aim of the business conference is to better align HR with business priorities and to identify opportunities to work better together. The purpose of the Team will be to act as an online workspace where HR and business can better co-design and co-create a conference experience that aligns to both their needs. It will also reduce the confusion that goes into planning such an event and minimise the email communications.

The name of the Team will be: FY20 Human Resource Conference.

People

People who will need access to the Team will all be internal stakeholders and members who will be coordinating the event:

- Key senior HR leaders
- Business unit heads
- Executive assistants to business unit leaders
- Business conference project Team members.

Priorities

- Identify a venue
- Develop a theme for the conference that aligns with the business strategy
- Identify and recruit speakers: keynote and session facilitator
- Work out logistics of transportation, accommodation and meals
- Manage conference registrations.

It is anticipated that the following channels be created around the above priorities:

- General (for general announcements)

- Conference Design and Speaking Plans (conversations on how we will structure the outline for the day)
- Guest Speakers (notes and conversations regarding guest speaker details)
- Venue Information (conversations around venue requirements and issues)
- Meals Information (conversations around meal requirements and issues)
- Transport Information (conversations around transport requirements and issues)
- Registration (conversations about the registration process)
- Post-Event Wrap-Up (conversations about the evaluation and wrap-up of the event).

Principles

- No emails will be sent to Team members, and all emails will be placed into the relevant channel
- The General channel will be reserved for Team-wide communication only
- 1:1 chat messages will only be used for one-to-one communications that are not relevant to the wider group
- Members will respond to posts where they are mentioned (@) by replying, liking, or mentioning others to keep the conversation going.

Plugins

The Team will require the following plugins:

- SharePoint tab to SharePoint Human Resources file store
- Website tab to access to Human Resources Intranet page
- Microsoft Forms tab (and associated form) for managing registrations
- Link to OneNote notebook for collaborative note taking and brainstorming.

Permissions

- This will be a Team for members only—not public
- No external guest access required
- Four Team Owners selected from the business and Human Resources
- Additional Team member access requested from the Team Owners for approval, especially as there will be files and resources that may have potentially sensitive and confidential personnel information.

Performance

- Reduce the amount of emails in our inbox to coordinate an event of this size
- Streamline the coordination effort for these annual events

- Identify collaborative projects between HR and business that can be put in place for the year against business goals and outcomes.

Provisioning

- We will need the support of IT to help set up the Teams via a ServiceNow request. Once we have the Team created, the Team Owner will create the channels and add the appropriate tabs.

Perishability

- As this is an annual event, we will keep this Team available as a reference for the next three years to assist in planning future events. Team owners will archive the team after the event so we can refer to it in the future. We anticipate that this Team will form a template for future conferences that HR will plan and coordinate.

REGIONAL SALES TEAM MEETINGS

Problem

We have twenty sales team members who are currently working in the regions and are responsible for serving customers who are long distances away from main cities or hubs. These sales agents are responsible for a geographical region and can organise and work according to their client needs as well as head office requirements.

Although sales agents use and access our Customer Relationship Management (CRM) system for all sales enquiries, referrals and servicing, the main form of communication between the sales team is via email or mobile phone. This results in a high burden of email traffic between the sales team members, especially when it comes to sharing information around customers, identifying opportunities for new products and services to be sold, and bringing in insights that could improve our customer service. Although the sales team is within European time zones, they also speak on the phone regularly, even when on the road. Considering the vast distances that they cover, we need a solution that will not only be a safer option on the road (so they're not checking emails and phone messages often) but also give them line of sight over what their peers in other regions are working on and areas of collaboration or knowledge sharing.

Purpose

The purpose of this Team is to be able to plan, prepare, and coordinate the various sales activities of our representatives in the field; identify areas of duplication; and obtain insights into potential new sales activities that can be undertaken in the regions. It is anticipated that our weekly national sales meetings will reduce in duration as the agents would have access to information in Microsoft Teams.

The name of the Team will be called "FY20 Northern Sales Territory."

People

- 20 × regional sales team agents
- National sales manager
- Head of business line customer service (sponsor)
- EA to head of business line customer service.

Priorities

- Sell more!
- Streamline the way we do our weekly sales meeting
- Get more focused on pipeline development and conversion into new customer opportunities

- Provide access to data to help our reps better manage their territory
- Improve the digital literacy of our sales team members when using our CRM.

It is anticipated that the following channels be created around the above priorities

- General (for announcements and broadcasts only)
- Weekly Sales Meetings (conversations and files for access for all weekly sales meetings)
- Issues and Concerns (conversations on issues and concerns identified in the field)
- New Opportunities (conversations on how to progress new opportunities and referrals)
- Regional Business Reports (conversations around weekly reports; what works and what can be improved)
- CRM Skills (conversations about how to use our CRM effectively).

Principles

- We will not use email to communicate with each other. Instead, all conversations are to happen in the relevant channel in Microsoft Teams.
- All emails received from our customers will be placed into the relevant channel for all to view
- New channels for conversation are to be forwarded for approval to the one of three Team Owners for consideration

- Weekly sales team meetings will include an agenda item on how we are using Microsoft Teams and what we can improve
- We will record all national sales team meetings within Microsoft Teams so that sales agents may view these at their convenience
- Major wins should be announced in the General channel so we can all celebrate each other's successes.

Plugins

The team will require the following plugins:

- Wiki for "How to Use this Team"
- Dynamics CRM Tab to access to CRM system in the CRM Skills channel
- No connectors or bots required
- SharePoint tab pointing to our product information and marketing packs.

Permissions

- Private Team for members only
- Three Team Owners identified from the sales teams
- No external guest access will be required.

Performance

- Reduce the amount of emails between head office, sales agents and customers
- Reduce the time spent on mobile phones, especially when driving
- Identify areas for new sales opportunities and referrals for our business
- Identify areas for co-operation between geographic regions
- Reduce the weekly sales team meeting duration from one hour to thirty minutes.

Provisioning

- As we have sales regions around the world, this isn't the first time this problem has occurred. We will use the templated Team structure already available via our Team request process.

Perishability

- Territories change regularly, so this Team is likely to be relevant only for the current financial year. Team owners will archive the Team after no communication or engagement has occurred in the channels for over three years and will advise Team members of its archiving.
- File management in accordance with our company IT policy.

BOARD AND COMMITTEE MEETINGS

Problem

We have various committees that report to our board members quarterly. Committees must follow a consistent process to ensure that adequate time is dedicated to decision-making and actions needed for the successful operation of our company. Although the formal nature of our committee meetings has supported us, we would like to explore ways to use a more collaborative and open approach to running these as well as an opportunity for committee members to actively discuss and debate items throughout the year, and not just at set times before board meetings.

Purpose

The purpose of this Team is to help board members to undertake their roles and responsibilities when planning, preparing, and presenting to the board. Another purpose is to ensure that items for discussion and review are available at any time and on any device.

People

- Committee members
- Board members
- EAs of board members

Priorities

- Establish clear schedule of meetings and agendas
- Consolidate the collation of board papers so that information is available to members at least three days prior to the meeting
- Enable our committee to meet virtually when necessary
- Track decisions and actions off the back of the meeting.

The channels of conversation may be:

- General (for announcements and broadcasts only)
- Terms of Reference (conversations about the scope of the committee)
- Board Meeting: January
- Board Meeting: April
- Board Meeting: July
- Board Meeting: October
- Standing Tasks and Actions (conversations on tasks and actions identified in committee meetings)

- On Hold (conversations on items held over).

Principles

- We will not use email to communicate with each other. Instead, all conversations are to happen in the relevant channel in Microsoft Teams
- All committee-related emails received (and sent) are to be copied into the relevant channel
- New channels for conversation are to be forwarded for approval to the Team Owners for consideration
- Committee meetings will be recorded in Microsoft Teams
- The committee Teams will be private Teams as conversations and files for discussions will be closed to the public
- We value open and transparent practices, and as such, we will provide a link to the recording of the committee meeting on Yammer for any employee to view and comment on.

Plugins

The team will require the following plugins:

- Wiki for "How We Work in this Committee" that highlights how we will work together and engage with each other online and on our board as well as our committee processes

- Word tab displaying the document that includes terms of reference of the committee
- Yammer tab which displays the organisation-facing Yammer community of the committee where key outcomes and the recording of the decisions of the committee are shared internally.

Permissions

- Private Team for members only
- Three Team owners identified from the committee secretariat
- No external guest access will be required.

Performance

- Improve and streamline our committee meetings
- Reduce the time it takes for new committee members to undertake their roles and responsibilities
- Build openness and transparency into our decision-making process.

Provisioning

- Work with IT to set up and structure the Microsoft Teams and channels—this can be templated for many committees across the organisation
- Work and coach committee members who may not be comfortable on camera

- Work with IT to consider how to have board meetings livestreamed through Microsoft Teams or Yammer in the long term.

Perishability

- File management and Team archival in accordance with the committee governance rules put in place by the company secretary and our company IT policy.

CUSTOMER SERVICE

Problem

We rely on a five-member staff made up of part-timers to service our internal business clients. Currently, as our team works at various times of the day and in shifts, information is lost, and we are unable to determine the state and progress of tasks and actions between team members. Messages are written on Post-it notes or pieces of paper that are left on the desk for the next rostered person to read and action; there's little consistency between how staff members work, and they are unable to find the files and documents of what's been worked on or what needs to be done.

We need more situational awareness so we can pick up where others have left off and be more informed of what we are all doing. This will help provide a more united front to our internal business clients.

Purpose

The purpose of this Team is to provide a more coherent and consistent approach to our work so that we present a united front to our stakeholders and internal customers and are able to give them peace of mind that their enquiry will be actioned.

The Team will be called "Customer Service Huddle."

People

- 5 × part-time staff members
- Team leader

Priorities

- Ensure that no inbound general enquiries fall between the cracks
- Provide a place to hand over the context of current cases
- Enable our team to get help from their peers when trying to answer questions
- Capture lessons learned from customer conversations

The channels of conversation may be:

- General: for announcements and broadcasts only
- Inbound for Action: enquiries that come in through our support email that need action, with the potential to automate this using Power Automate (Flow) in near future

- Handoff: to provide context to the next customer service agent on shift/link to the job in our customer service system
- How Do I...?: conversations on questions around how Team members undertake processes for knowledge sharing
- Ideas for Workflow Improvement: conversations on ideas for improving workflow through automating or streamlining process
- Today I Learned: conversations around sharing tips and techniques for better handling customer interactions.

Principles

- We will not use email to communicate with each other. Instead, all conversations are to happen in the relevant channel in Microsoft Teams.
- When we learn something new, we will go into the "Today I Learned" channel and set up a meeting to share the lesson. This meeting that explains the improved process will be recorded and made available for the rest of the Team or new starters to watch at a time that is convenient.

Plugins

The team will require the following plugins:

- Wiki for "How We Work in this Team" that highlights how we will work together and engage with each other online in the Team
- Zendesk tab to list all current tickets the Team is currently working on
- Link to collaborative OneNote Notebook.

Permissions

- Private Team for members only
- Two Team owners identified
- No external guest access will be required.

Performance

- Reduce time taken to respond to customer enquiries
- Build consistent and coherent "one team" approach in our workflow
- Reduce the time it takes to find, manage, and share information
- Receive a 90% or higher satisfaction rating in our customer servicing evaluation form
- Identify areas where our work can be streamlined or automated to become at least 20% more efficient.

Provisioning

- Work with IT to set up and structure the Microsoft Teams and channels

- Work and coach Team members on online communication, collaboration, and sharing behaviours
- Provide more hands-on coaching and support to those members who need it the most.

Perishability

- Every three months, we will curate the best conversations and turn them into a document, ensuring that new starters joining the Team can quickly get up to speed
- File management and Team archival will be conducted in accordance with the committee governance rules put in place by the company secretary and our company IT policy.

1:1 / EMPLOYEE EXPERIENCE

Problem

I manage a team of nine people, and as per company policy, I need to facilitate a 1:1 conversation with each of my direct reports, at least once per month. Currently those meetings occur face-to-face in our meeting room, and I take notes in my traditional, paper-based notebook. That's right, with no technology. Shock, horror – I know! I keep these notes to myself. Every six months, I conduct a formal performance review with each of my team members. After that review, I need to update our HR performance management system, which is a web-based application (and I can never remember the address). My team continuously ask questions about learning and development and career progression throughout the year; however, the resources are strewn all over our corporate intranet. A lot of the answers are available via these resources; however, my team keep coming to me for the answers. This takes what should be a quick 1:1 chat and turns it into a lengthy process.

Purpose

To create a space where I can consolidate all aspects of my team member's "employee experience," making it easy for my team to engage in productive 1:1 conversations and helping me better manage expectations based on company policy. This space could move with the employee as they change roles within our organisation, creating a consistent experience for them throughout their employment journey.

The Team will be called "Employee Experience: <first name> <last name>", and I will create one for each of my 9 direct reports.

People

- Myself
- The relevant direct report

Priorities

- Make sure we consistently engage in and document our 1:1 conversations
- Consider learning and development opportunities as they present themselves
- Create a space for each member of my team to raise issues or challenges privately

The channels of conversation may be:

- General (where we will store important employment-related documentation, like the position description)
- 1:1s (where we schedule our recurring monthly 1:1 conversation – which could happen face to face, or via Teams video call. Actions and updates can be provided in this channel in between 1:1 conversations)
- Learning and Development (where we will co-create the training plan)
- What needs fixing (a safe space where my Team member can raise any issue that may need attention).

Principles

- Don't wait for our 1:1. Post ideas, action items or issues directly into the Team as they happen
- Share notes from each 1:1 in the 1:1 channel within 24 hours of the conversation.

Plugins

- Website tab to access the HR Performance Management system (added to the 1:1 channel)
- Website tabs to link to corporate policies and learning resources relevant to our 1:1 conversations
- Stream tab in the Learning and Development channel linking to the playlist of compliance training that all our team members need to watch.

Permissions

- Private Team for just the two participants in the employment relationship, and our HR Business Partner
- The Director of our division may join the Team in circumstances where formal performance management processes have been initiated.

Performance

- Ultimately the performance of this Team will be measured through our employee satisfaction survey, specifically the questions relating to the performance management and learning and development processes.

Provisioning

- We will use the templated Employee Experience Team available via the IT service desk. I hear a rumour that next year these Teams will be automatically provisioned for every manager across the organisation. This will include tabs already set up with the important resources my Team regularly asks me about.

Perishability

- As this is a record of a team member's employment with our organisation, we need to retain this Team for seven years after they leave our organisation (as per the *State Archives Act*) .

NEXT STEPS

By now we hope you have created (or at least have the inspiration for) the perfect space for your team to come together and achieve more using Microsoft Teams.

The next few weeks will be important as you start to bring your team on the Microsoft Teams journey. As an executive, manager, or team leader, you can "make or break" how your team embraces this new way of working. Your direct reports will look to you to lead by example and will make decisions as to how they use Microsoft Teams, based on the signals you provide. Here are a few simple things that you can do to ensure that the change you are leading your team through can be sustainable in the long term:

- Try to avoid sending emails where possible. Instead:
    - For quick responses, send a chat message
    - For topics that everyone should be aware of or be able to respond to, post your message into the most appropriate Team and channel
    - If someone asks you a question via email, forward that email to the most appropriate Team and channel and reply to the email within Teams so everyone can see your response

- Stop emailing attachments. If you want to share a document with one person, share the file using the chat feature; if all of your team should be able to see/review/respond to your document, post it into the most appropriate Team
- Don't just pick up the phone; have a video call instead (*no matter how much you don't like your face on camera!*)
- Make sure your regular in-person or distributed team meeting is set up with a "Microsoft Teams meeting" included; this will enable people to be able to join your team meeting from any location (not just the meeting room in your office).

With just a handful of changes in the way that you communicate, collaborate, and coordinate, you will see your team embrace new ways of working in no time.

"Microsoft Teams Is Great…How Do We Bring the Rest of Our Organisation Along for the Ride?"

Firstly, we recommend you "pay it forward" and share your copy of this book with one of your colleagues. The more advocates for this new way of working within your organisation (especially in executive or management layers), the greater the impact on your success. If you need more paperback copies of this book to distribute to your entire management team, go to https://teamsbook.info and use the code "IHaveReadTheBook" to get 10% off and free shipping on any bulk order of 30 copies or more.

Secondly, capture the success that your team has had with Microsoft Teams and turn it into an internal case study. The case study or "exemplar story" doesn't have to be very detailed—one page or a quick video will do. Make sure you capture the problem you are solving, the purpose of your Team, and the people you are collaborating with. Share your priorities and document your wins. Your story will become the evidence of success that your peers look for when trying to make sense of how to unlock value from Microsoft Teams. As more of your colleagues and their teams jump on board, make sure you collate all your success stories and make them accessible to your organisation.

Thirdly, if you are ready to launch Microsoft Teams at scale, take advantage of the guidance that is available to you and your organisation. Microsoft has produced several guides to help you land Microsoft Teams across your organisation. We have included links to those resources in the appendix of this book, but you could start with https://aka.ms/TeamsAdoption.

At *Adopt & Embrace*, we work with our customers in Australia and New Zealand to help their workforces embrace Microsoft Teams like no other program. At the time of writing, we have helped over 350,000 people unlock value from Microsoft 365, every single month.

Even though we are based in our special part of the Southern Hemisphere, you can take advantage of our "secret sauce," no matter where you are in the world. It is all available via our digital platform—the *Adopt & Embrace Academy*.

If you are serious about launching Microsoft Teams across your organisation, make sure you take advantage of our 14-step adoption roadmap, "done for you" resources, and supportive community of adoption, change management, business improvement, and project management professionals from around the world who are working towards the same goals you are.

You can learn more about the *Adopt & Embrace Academy*, and try it out with our *"$7 for 7 days"* trial at https://adoptandembrace.academy.

Still Need Guidance?

The best performers in sport, music, and business almost always have a coach in their corner. Let our award-winning team guide you through your specific Microsoft Teams (and Office 365) adoption challenges to help you achieve both your professional and personal goals, just like we already have for hundreds of customers across the world.

Want to make sure the rest of your organisation unlocks value from Microsoft Teams? We can come to you and facilitate onsite workshops with people across your organisation to create the perfect Team for their needs.

Whether it is via a Teams video call, in-person strategy, co-design or coaching workshops, our Adoption Consultants can help your workforce understand and take advantage of the potential at their fingertips with Microsoft Teams and the rest of the Microsoft 365 platform.

Learn more about how engaging *Adopt & Embrace* at your organisation can help you unlock real business value at https://www.adoptandembrace.com. Or get in touch at engage@adoptandembrace.com.

APPENDIX:
MICROSOFT TEAMS RESOURCES

L ong gone are the days of software being shipped with volumes of manuals, user guides, and pages of shortcut keys. In fact, we are old enough to remember when you used to get those plastic guides that fit neatly on top your keyboard to tell you what all the function keys did.

The problem with printed material (including this book) is that we live in a world where software is changing rapidly. Because of this constant state of A/B testing, feature releases and user interface improvements, we purposefully wrote this book to focus on the fundamentals of Microsoft Teams and how to put those fundamentals to good use. As we write this book, there isn't a month that goes by where there isn't a new feature, new capability, or new industry-specific configuration of Microsoft Teams. It is hard for us to keep up, let alone those people who don't live and breathe Microsoft Teams. In fact, we had to time the release of the book to align with Microsoft's annual technology conference, *Ignite,* to ensure we included some of the more recent product updates (sorry to our editors, who felt the full force of these last-minute amendments!).

So, where are the best places to keep on top of what is happening with Microsoft Teams? Where are the trusted references or resources that you and your team can rely on when you want to introduce a new starter to Microsoft Teams or dive deep into how to automate numerous business processes by building software solutions on top of Microsoft Teams?

Below is our list of favourite resources. The list is not exhaustive; however, it will provide you with a broad library of resources that you can look to as you continue on your Microsoft Teams journey.

- End User Training for Microsoft Teams https://aka.ms/TeamsEndUserTraining
- Everyday Etiquette in Microsoft Teams (AvePoint) https://www.avepoint.com/ebook/microsoft-teams-best-practices
- Microsoft Teams UserVoice (to provide feedback/submit feature requests) https://aka.ms/TeamsFeedback
- Microsoft 365 adoption resources, including the Office 365 Champions Program and other resources https://aka.ms/MicrosoftAdoption
- Driving Adoption group in the Microsoft Tech Community https://aka.ms/DriveAdoption

Finally, make sure you visit https://teamsbook.info and click on "Resources" to access the workbook that accompanies this book, and other curated resources we discover.

GLOSSARY

Bot
Bots (short for robots) perform simple and repetitive tasks that allow you to obtain information from another website. Microsoft Teams has bots that you can use (like the "Who" bot) to find an expert in your business, or you can develop your own.

Lync
Lync was the early name of the product that became Skype for Business.

Microsoft Partner
Microsoft Partners are a global network of Microsoft certified independent companies and individuals who offer Microsoft-related products and services

Microsoft Stream
Microsoft Stream is an enterprise video platform where users can upload, host, and share company video assets securely (think of it as a "Corporate YouTube").

Microsoft Word

Microsoft Word is Microsoft's word processing software package.

Office 365 Portal

The Office 365 portal at https://portal.office.com is where you can access all your Office 365 services.

SharePoint

SharePoint is Microsoft's collaborative server environment, which allows for the creation of websites and sharing of data and documents within a company.

Social Learning

Social learning is learning with others to make sense of and create new ideas. Learning can be augmented with social media tools that allow people to connect and collaborate on any work project, interest or skill. It is seen as the fundamental shift in how people work and leveraging tools and resources that allow connections and collaborations to happen within the flow of their work.

Wiki

A wiki is an online space' where users can add and edit content collaboratively.

REFERENCES

Appelo, J. (2017, May 12). *How to Define and Evolve Your Team Principles*. Retrieved from Agility Scales: https://blog.agilityscales.com/how-to-define-and-evolve-your-team-principles-81bc2589ba0c.

Bos, N., Gergle, D., Olson, J., & Olson, G. (2001). Being there versus seeing there: Trust via video. *CHI '01 Extended Abstracts on Human Factors in Computing Systems*. New York: ACM.

Brookfield, S. (1988). *Training Educators of Adults*. New York: Routledge.

Cameron, A., & Webster, J. (2005). Unintended consequences of emerging communication technologies: Instant messaging in the workplace. *Computers in Human Behavior* 21, 85–103.

Chugh, R. (2015). Do Australian universities encourage tacit knowledge transfer? *Proceedings of the 7th International Joint Conference on Knowledge Discovery, Knowledge Engineering and Knowledge Management* (pp. 128–135). Lisbon.

Leinwand, P., & Mainardi, C. (2011, April 14). Stop chasing too many priorities. *Harvard Business Review*. Retrieved from HBR.org: https://hbr.org/2011/04/stop-chasing-too-many-prioriti.

Mark, G., Gudith, D., & Klocke, U. (2008). The cost of interrupted work: More speed and stress. *CHI '08 Proceedings of the SIGCHI Conference on Human Factors in Computing Systems*. Florence: ACM.

Mehrabian, A. (1971). *Silent Messages.* Belmont: Wadsworth.

Nguyen, D., & Canny, J. (2007). MultiView: Improving trust in group video conferencing through spatial faithfulness. *Proceedings of the 2007 Conference on Human Factors in Computing Systems.* San Jose: CHI 2007.

Rigg, C., & Trehan, K. (2008). Critical reflection in the workplace: Is it just too difficult? *Journal of European Industrial Training* 32(5), 374–384.

Ringelmann, M. (1913). Recherches sur les moteurs animés: Travail de l'homme. *Annales de l'Insitut National Agronomique* 12, 1–40.

Sinek, S. (2009, September). How great leaders inspire action. *TEDxPuget Sound.* Seattle, WA, United States: TED. Retrieved from https://www.ted.com/talks/simon_sinek_how_great_leaders_inspire_action

Sinek, S. (2011). *Start With Why.* New York: Portfolio Trade.

Stolovich, H.D., & Keeps, E.J. (2004). *Training Ain't Performance.* ASTD Press.

Udemy Research. (2018). *Udemy in Depth: 2018 Workplace Distraction Report.* Retrieved from Udemy Research: https://research.udemy.com/research_report/udemy-depth-2018-workplace-distraction-report/.

Wenger, E., Trayner, B., & de Laat, M. (2011). *Promoting and Assessing Value Creation in Communities and Networks: A Conceptual Framework.* Ruud de Moor Centrum.

ACKNOWLEDGEMENTS

Writing a book takes more than just an author, or authors. It takes a team, a community to help craft, shape, refine, validate and embrace the ideas or concepts that end up in printed form. We (Paul, Helen, Benjamin, and Darrell) could not have published this book without the help of the following people.

Firstly, our amazing customers at *Adopt & Embrace*, the willing participants as we have experimented with and refined our thinking over the past few years when it comes to Microsoft Teams Design. We are proud of the outcomes that you have been able to achieve using Microsoft Teams, improving employee and customer experiences while reducing waste from your business processes. Here's to many more breakthroughs into the future.

Secondly, the people inside the machine at Microsoft who have championed, coached, and supported our team as we work to amplify the impact of Microsoft Teams and the rest of Microsoft 365 with our customers. In no particular order: Wayne Lewis, Ginny Hoban, Chris Large, Karuana Gatimu, Joanna Boxrud, Sandy Walker, Olga Gordon, Arbindo Chattopadhyay, Vakhtang Assatrian, Jason La Greca, Matt Goddard, Hao Tang, Steve Green, Matt Ontell, Manfred Cheng, Phil Goldie, Brooke Galloway, Scott Turner, Evan Williams, Jas Basra, Amanda Le, Sarah Arnold, Kristina Jamieson-Penn, Kim Haines, and the dozens of Microsoft One Commercial Partner and field team members with whom we co-sell every day.

Thirdly, to the people who helped us put this book together. Our book coaches Cathryn Mora and Veronica McDermott who guided us from concept, to finished draft, to published work. To our beta readers—Joanna Teirney, Reid Skinner, Sandy Breadsell, Paul Colmer, Kelli Boultbee, Mathew Gilbertson, Luis Suarez, Rebecca Zhang, Lia Cragnolini, Rebecca Westall, Marianne Bae, Rene Modery, Eoin Connors, Kelly Doyle, Melinda Grant, Renetta Alexander, Loryan Strant, Andrew Jolly, Gro Elin Hansen, and Zarina Bakhaeva—who took our unedited thoughts and helped us to ensure they made sense outside of our heads as well.

Finally, to the rest of team at *Adopt & Embrace*—Nicole Short, Jenni McNamara, Jeff Bell, John Tropea, Maddy Dunn and Kerrina Woods. Thank you for your contributions to many of the ideas presented in this book, your patience as we focused on the writing process, and your support as we grow *Adopt & Embrace* together. Special thanks to Athanasia Price, who is no longer with our team, but was instrumental in helping us get this project off the ground.

ABOUT THE AUTHORS

Paul Woods

Paul Woods is the Founder of *Adopt & Embrace*. *Adopt & Embrace* focuses on helping people get their day back through sustainable, relevant, and focused adoption of Microsoft 365 that results in real business outcomes. *Adopt & Embrace* was announced as a 2018 Microsoft Global Partner of the year after just two years and nine months of operation. This came after *Adopt & Embrace* was named a Microsoft Australia Partner of the Year in 2016, after just nine months of operation.

Before staring *Adopt & Embrace* in 2015, Paul held various marketing and management roles at a major Australian Microsoft Partner, and was a Technology Specialist at Microsoft Australia. He recently completed research as part of the *Work/Industry Futures Research Program* at the Queensland University of Technology, focusing on technology-enabled mobile work and the porosity of work/life borders. He has also been a member of the teaching team at the QUT Business School for Strategic Management and Negotiation Across Borders.

Awarded Microsoft's Most Valuable Professional (MVP) award ten times, Paul is a regular speaker at community-based events as well as at regional and global Microsoft Conferences like *Microsoft TechEd*, *Microsoft Ignite: The Tour*, and *Microsoft Inspire*.

Find him on Twitter as @paulwoods or on LinkedIn at https://www.linkedin.com/in/paulwoods.

Helen Blunden

Helen Blunden is the Community Manager for *Adopt & Embrace* and has over 23 years of experience in learning and development across private, public, and not-for-profit organisations. With a specialty in performance consulting and informal learning, she believes that organisations need to help their employees build new skills to navigate through a complex world of constant change.

Helen has a passion for enabling people to learn beyond the traditional tools. She believes in the power of networks and communities supported by social tools that drive collaboration, meaning, and engagement in the work.

Helen believes that the "learning is the work and the work is the learning," meaning that the tools are instruments that enable us to connect with peers who can inspire us with fresh new ideas, allowing us to apply them to our own personal or professional contexts.

With experience across all forms of learning, from facilitator-led instruction, online and blended, virtual and social, she practices what she preaches. She is an active user of social tools and emerging technologies and uses these with her clients to put the fun, exploration, and curiosity back into learning.

Find her on Twitter as @activatelearn or on LinkedIn at https://www.linkedin.com/in/helenblunden.

Benjamin Elias

Benjamin Elias is a Senior Adoption Specialist at *Adopt & Embrace* and has been awarded Most Valuable Professional by Microsoft in the Office Apps & Services category.

Passionate about creativity and innovation, he plays where humans and technology intersect. Benjamin started off life as an engineer, completed a psychology major, went to work for a bank, ran a SaaS start-up, and now combines all those experiences to help people use technology more effectively at work.

His journey into the Microsoft world started as a citizen developer with Yammer apps after becoming interested in the social networking tool. He has since been invited to speak at Build 2019, Microsoft's premier developer conference, about a Teams app he developed which used artificial intelligence to organise team coffee orders. As the only person in the team who can code, he gets given special projects with surprising regularity.

Find him on Twitter as @collabital or on LinkedIn at https://www.linkedin.com/in/bnelias/.

Darrell Webster

Darrell Webster has been helping organisations achieve more with Microsoft products for over 13 years. He provides change management and user adoption services to help IT projects see practical success, meeting the needs of the people they serve. He has been awarded a Microsoft MVP award each year since 2013, in recognition of his contributions to the Microsoft Technical Community.

Darrell is also a co-founder of and contributor to Regarding 365, a community of content creators sharing experiences, opinions, and advice for the Microsoft 365 collection of cloud-productivity services.

Learn more by visiting www.regarding365.com and on Darrell's YouTube channel at www.youtube.com/darrellasaservice.

DFind him on Twitter as @darrellaas or on LinkedIn at https://www.linkedin.com/in/darrellwebster/.